MEDITATIVE FITNESS

- man
- Patients
- Yoga
- stairs
- nightsweats

Transform fitness, transform life.

MEDITATIVE FITNESS
The Art and Practice of the Workout

Clark Hamilton Depue

ISBN-13: 9780692562031
ISBN-10: 0692562036
Library of Congress Control Number: 2015917808
Sparkananda Press, Irving, TX

To our hearts and souls
awakening and finding peace,
to the light and good
in each of us.
To any of you that have ever
struggled to be happy,
live in your truth,
and follow your path.
To the lifting of suffering,
to love, peace, and joy.
To kindness in the world,
caring in our hearts,
and miracles within.

Contents

The Processes

▲▼▲▼▲

Introduction   199
The Foundation   207

Pre-Workout   237

The Workout 258

Post-Workout 269

Mantras and Affirmations 281

Acknowledgements

I AM ETERNALLY grateful to my mother, Cheri, for her love and heart that have been a blessing in my life; to my father, David, for his love and spirit; you have both been beautiful examples for me to become the man I am today; to Donna, Gaga, my sister Lacey and nephews Landon, Tristan, and Jackson, I love you all very much; you all helped set this chain of events in motion, and this book is for all of you as well.

I wish to express my deepest gratitude to James Thorne III and Scott Pagliaccio for being who you are and for sharing in this vision. You guys helped give life to this book. To Becky Owens, thank you for everything you did to help this book on it's journey. To Sara Cassidy, thank you for helping this book continue to rise. The process astounds me; thank you all for helping this miracle see the light.

I extend a special thank you to Nicholas Wilton, whose art was with me from the beginning. I'll always remember the day you joined us, how the book rose to a new level. Your presence helped guide this as a work of art. Thank you, Laila Rezai and Danielle Cloe, for your beautiful artistry as well, and Kiley Freshwater Evans, for being there at the end of this long journey.

Thank you, Allie and Stella, my girls who were with me every step of the way and who play a significant role; and Xander, wherever you are, I love you little buddy. Thank you for the gifts you bring my heart.

I would like to honor and send love to everyone who has made a difference on this journey, including everyone at Tiger's Den and everyone I served with and know through Pathways Core Training. Thank you for your love and support, and for sharing your hearts that have taught me so much – your hearts are in this book as well. To all of my former students, whom I cherish; to my friends Richard and Ale, Mark, Brad, Frank, and all my friends over the years who will always be dear friends; to all those with whom I have connected or shared a moment on this journey; to all the angels who helped guide my path, including Angie White, Teresi Cole, Zhanna Soli, and Patti Villalobos; to all who have offered their love and encouragement: Gregg Manning, Clayton Smith, Kevin Wheeler, David and Jess Bynum, Harmony McKnight, Craig and Savanna Kwieren, Jill and Jeff Kunkle, Terry Srock, Ryan Lynn, Jason Thompson, Debbie Wright, my cousin Eliza, my neighbors, my dear friends in India, Devendra and Simbar, and so many others, thank you all for the blessings you have been.

I want to acknowledge all spiritual authors, teachers, thinkers, and masters who have come before and who are in the world; all who are spreading light, doing good in the world; all who are following their dreams and passions; all who have been an inspiration; and to all who read this, I love you all.

Definitions

THE FOLLOWING DEFINITIONS were realized to group concepts and broaden or specify meanings. Defined for the purpose of the book, when these words are used throughout the text, they appear in italic font and are understood with the following interpretations. As you enter the world of *meditative fitness*, it will help to familiarize yourself with them. Welcome to...

meditative fitness
1. The spiritual practice of fitness, the inner world of physical exertion.
2. The art of applying meditative elements to your fitness and the movement of your body; a meditative, metaphysical (beyond physical) approach to fitness.
3. A method for change and growth.

the practice
1. A *meditative fitness* practice, including your physical practice and journey of growth — *the workout*, meditation, mobility work, nutrition, and any other fitness or spiritual work.

2. Ongoing in nature, a way of engaging life from a place of learning, observing your inner world, open for self-realization – applying meditative and spiritual principles for the purpose of happiness, awakening, and enlightening.

3. Working toward mastery in any area of your life.

the four key areas (of being)

Mind, body, heart, and soul, corresponding with the mental, physical, emotional, and spiritual.

the foundation

The base of your practice, the groundwork that creates easily accessible pathways, inner connections, and the ability to enter a *meditative state* with ease or even a single breath. *The foundation* taught here includes relaxation, *pure intention,* connecting to your breath and energy, engaging your heart, and tuning in to your body.

meditative state

A relaxed mind, body, and central nervous system, slower brainwaves, a deeper state of heart and mind, a transcendent state of being. Relaxed, yet alert and focused with intention, presence, and awareness. This state can be entered in an instant, a breath, or over time. It can also be entered and exited repeatedly, going deeper each time. This is the state to incorporate in and around *the workout.*

go in(side)

Entering a *meditative state,* tuning in, an inner state of awareness, often beginning with closing one's eyes.

pure intention

1. A meditative form of intention, pure-hearted, flowing and allowing. We embody *pure intention* in a meditative workout and in meditative processes such as clearing energy or visualization.
2. An absolute belief, focus, and expectation, knowing an outcome, seeing through and overriding doubts.
3. A determination and will that moves your body, moves the weights, and propels you through *the workout.*

inner senses

Metaphysical senses, tuning in and sensing (hearing, seeing, and feeling) from within – thoughts, emotion, energy, intuition, inner wisdom, and connection with a higher power. *Inner senses* help create your reality as well as physical strength and athletic movement.

the workout

1. Any form of physical exertion.
2. A series of *skills, lifts,* and *movements,* including strength training, skill work, and cardio or metcons (metabolic conditioning). i.e., part of a fitness regimen: CrossFit®, weightlifting, yoga, spin, attending group classes, going

to your local gym, cycling, running, walking, dancing, or playing sports.

3. As part of a *meditative fitness* practice, *the workout* is the meditation.

skill(s), lift(s), and movement(s)

The different types of exercises that typically make up *the workout*, often executed in various combinations and repetitions.

the challenge

1. An important element of life and *the workout*.
2. A level of difficulty unique to the individual, a test of ability, stepping out of one's comfort zone. *The challenge* leads to wisdom, adaptation, and growth. Physical challenges lead to the mental, emotional, and spiritual side of the equation, sparking thoughts, emotion, and other aspects of your inner world to move through in your practice.

the call(ing)

1. An inner summoning, intuition, or whisper from within.
2. Being drawn to rise to *the challenge*, live in your truth, and face the path that lies before you. The choice is whether to answer *the call* of life and *the workout*.

fitness karma

Everything that has come before that you now carry in your present, all the causes and effects that have led to who you are now in relation to your fitness – your cumulative knowledge and perspective, sports and fitness experience, strengths and weaknesses, workout styles, food and nutrition, body mobility, and injuries or ailments.

rest (period)

The time recovering your strength or your breath and heart rate in *the workout* – the time preparing to go back to work. In strength training, the time between sets of repetitions. Short *rests* are ideal meditative opportunities during *the workout*.

the breath

1. A single breath or the collective act of breathing.
2. The air that enters and leaves *the body*.
3. A catalyst for working with your energy, and one of your greatest resources in meditation and *the workout*.

core breath

1. A deep breath starting in your diaphragm, expanding to your chest, ending with a full exhale, exercising full lung capacity.
2. A breath that helps brace your core in *skills, lifts,* and *movements*.
3. Breathing at the center of being in meditation.

anchor

A trigger for memory or a specific state or feeling. *Anchors* happen naturally in our everyday lives, and we can also set empowering *anchors* for ourselves. For example, a song that brings up a memory is an *anchor* for that experience. A hand or finger position practiced in meditation can be an *anchor* for relaxation and a *meditative state. The breath* and different types of breaths can be powerful *anchors* in meditation and *the workout.*

the body

An expression of heart, mind, and being, reflecting your inner world, values, love, and care. The spiritual body (also known as the celestial, astral, metaphysical, or energy body) is the life and energy in and around the physical form. The physical body is the ultimate instrument, allowing us to infinitely play and create and experience the physical world. *Meditative fitness* as a spiritual practice is the divine merging and integration of the physical and spiritual bodies.

enlightening emotion

1. A productive expression and movement through your feelings without judgment, wallowing, or self-created suffering.
2. Keeping an open heart, connecting with your soul, divine truth, higher vision, and heart-level intelligence.
3. Emotion that is uplifting in nature, such as love, peace, joy, strength, courage, gratitude, forgiveness, and compassion.

abnormalities

Any one or many of the following: tired, cloudy, heavy, or low energy, indigestion, emotional instability and moodiness, excessive inflammation, chronic knots and tight muscles, inflamed fascia, tendonitis, muscle cramps, shortness of breath, painful bloating and other stomach pains, excessive gas, inflamed bowels, inconsistent bowel movements, joint and back pain, headaches, and other body aches.

the new normal

Feeling magnificent, awake with an abundance of energy, a sense of well-being, *the body* at peace with no *abnormalities*. *The new normal* is when your body is in harmony with everything you put into it, digesting with ease and smooth, consistent bowel movements. *The new normal* is a sharp mind, clear body, and light spirit. *The new mobility normal* is when *the body* and joints are able to move pain-free with full ranges of motion – *the body* at peace in movement.

Preface

IF YOU HAVE ever worked out a day in your life, if you love fitness or want to learn to love fitness, or if you want to improve your relationship with yourself and your body, this book is for you. If you want more depth and light in your life, if you want to overcome challenges and raise your state of being, or if you've ever felt like fitness contributes to your happiness and is part of your spiritual life, you will love what is in store for you.

This book has the potential to change your perspective of fitness. For some, it will be a wonderful validation. For others, it will be an eye-opening and enlightening experience. If you are not currently exercising in any form, then as you read this, embark on a journey of creating a physical practice – your own practice of *meditative fitness.* It starts right now, and it continues as soon as you engage in physical exertion. Set the intention, take action, and experience it for yourself. Make an appointment with yourself to exercise in whatever form you choose. Let the journey begin and start with whatever you can. See how good it feels to move; no need to waste the gift of physical life. If you so choose, you can stop reading right now and go for a walk or run. Spend some time stretching and mobilizing your body. Do as many pushups, sit-ups, squats, or lunges as you can. You can search online for proper form or standards of movement to ensure safety and maximum benefit. You can do any simple bodyweight *movement* and challenge yourself in very little time no matter where you are. The act of getting started generates momentous energy.

If you are currently engaging in some type of fitness regimen, you may recognize things you are already doing that make your fitness a living, breathing, active meditation. This is *Meditative Fitness: The Art and Practice of the Workout,* and you are in some ways already engaging in *the practice.* At the same time, you can set the intention for new meditative workout experiences. *Meditative fitness* is about movement of *the body* as well as movement of the heart and spirit. It is about reaching higher performance through spiritual practice. It is about the stuff that goes on inside of you as you go through a workout or as you practice living a healthy life. We will examine the non-physical side of fitness, our inner worlds, as we exert ourselves physically. This practice isn't meant to take a lot of time and effort in addition to what you are already doing. It is not something you force. It is something that simply is, something through which you allow intuition and inner wisdom to help guide you.

Meditative fitness happens when going to your local workout facility meets timeless spiritual practice. The lines become so beautifully blurred as you take things you are already doing and merge them with your spiritual life. *Meditative fitness* will change the way you approach your fitness, and *the workout* will never be the same. Taking care of yourself and leading a healthy life has much higher implications than the physical. By reading this, you are participating in the spiritual fitness revolution that is taking place.

Meditative Fitness is not a fitness program, but rather a way to engage your fitness. Rather than prescribe workouts, we prescribe meditative concepts and processes to apply to your workouts. This book is intended to complement all fitness programs and practices. It is intended to help transform your fitness into something even more extraordinary than it may already be.

Spiritual practice helps us lead happier and more fulfilling lives. It is the practice of being happy, of connecting with something deeper within ourselves, and connecting with what truly matters. To many of you, this may sound like the role fitness plays in your life. Spiritual practice is a way of life, a way of engaging life, something you do, the practice of your faith. Do you pray? Meditate? Practice yoga? Do you work out? Do you engage in uplifting activities? Do you talk to God? Do you listen carefully? Do you take a moment to breathe? Are you kind, caring, understanding, and loving toward yourself and others?

This book was also written to teach and broaden the way we see meditation, offering a new variety of *meditative fitness*. It was written to offer enough for you to build your unique and personal practice, to spark ongoing processing and self-realization, and to open the doors of your heart, mind, body, and soul.

At times, I will ask you questions, not always requiring an external or even conscious answer, but questions that rest in your subconscious and help guide you along the way, questions to repeat over the course of your life, to always be asking underneath, questions that your inner wisdom will help answer.

Within each of us resides our own truth, answers, and know-ingness. When we sincerely and vulnerably ask ourselves the big questions, they spark inner dialogue, which leads to new con-nections and deeper or heightened processing. At times, you may find value in reading the questions aloud. Trust your intuition to know when to do so. The text was written to speak to your inner guidance. Your subconscious will absorb more than your conscious mind. May you find new connections pop up in your consciousness at just the right time, perhaps in the middle of a workout, in the form of a realization or "aha" moment. May you find yourself effortlessly doing all the things your heart purely desires. May you connect with love for your body, love for the way you are, and love for your life. The heart of this book is for you to lead your most happy and soulfully fulfilling life.

The book has two parts: the chapters and the processes. The chapters consist of story elements and teaching elements. Each chapter conveys the essence of the subject, the overall understand-ing, how it relates to meditation and fitness, and how it applies in a meditative workout. The chapters are where you read about it, and the processes are where you take action – this is where you are doing it, experiencing it for yourself, and finding answers for your-self. The processes are where you will develop your own medita-tive techniques and build your practice, designed for the purpose of higher performance and personal growth. Specific processes are provided for reference at the end of chapters, corresponding to the material to enhance and deepen your understanding.

For your health and safety, please use your utmost wise discernment and seek the guidance of professionals as needed.

Listen to your body and take care of your body. You are the one who knows and governs your own safety. Listen to your intuition and apply discretion, because only you can fully govern your individual health and safety. Challenge and push yourself on an increasing gradient, knowing that you are capable of more than you think you are. Find the balance between pushing your limits and being safe. Be diligent in working on your movement, biomechanics, and mobility. Staying healthy is of the utmost importance for you to continue your practice. As it should, safety comes first in all physical training.

To get the most out of this book, test concepts for yourself. Add new meditative elements to your daily workouts. Complete the processes at the end of each chapter. And you can always begin your practice with the first small step – close your eyes and breathe.

If you don't have a meditative coach, guide, or teacher, you will need to get creative and take initiative. When you are in a meditation, if there is something you would like to do or accomplish, you can do so with creativity, initiative, and your powerful intention.

If you already have a meditation practice, take what's here, make it your own, and apply all of your meditation and *fitness karma* to your workouts.

This is a book of awareness, each chapter bringing awareness to its respective subject. The processes and questions serve to further raise your awareness. Not having answers leads to processing and realization. The best thing you can do is allow the questions to sink in. And any time you struggle, new awareness is right around the corner. Trust that you have the answers deeper within, and trust that clarity will appear.

The vision and teachings go beyond the bounds of this book. You can find out more and sign up to receive free bonus material at *MeditativeFitness.com,* including material to expand on concepts in the book and additional applications for your workouts and practice.

I would personally love to hear from you and share in your *meditative fitness* experiences, and so would everyone involved in bringing this book to light. Most of all, I care about your heart and soul and seek to be of service to your highest self. If there is something specific you would like me to address or expand on, such as an issue you face or a section or line in this book, please send me a message through our site, *MeditativeFitness.com,* dedicated to *meditative fitness* practitioners and the spiritually inclined.

Above all, love on, and enjoy the journey.

0

The Practice

⎯⎯⎯⎯⎯ ∽ ⎯⎯⎯⎯⎯

THERE ARE MANY spiritual and fitness related tales for where all of this began, but the book itself was born on a Saturday in September. Two days beforehand, three dreamers intersected for a universal collision and manifestation for the benefit of all. My dear friend James, who we all know as J.D., had been encouraging me for months to come see the new gym he opened and maybe even participate in a workout. When I finally stopped in, it happened to be on God's time.

My entire life, I knew I would one day write something, and for many years, I knew my life was headed down a spiritual path. A couple of weeks prior to this visit, I experienced a significant shift in my spiritual life, one that both changed and affirmed my path. With all veils of doubt lifted and intuitions confirmed, I knew the direction of my life, the direction I had always been headed. Again and again, everything made sense, and I knew what I was to do – find a way to teach meditation.

On my way over to see J.D., I must have known I was about to get a big hint on the Universe's surprise, for as I allowed my mind to journey in thought, envisioning what the gym would look like, I saw groups gathering for meditation. I wondered if they ever did that. Gazing into the future, I could see and feel the possibility, the karmic alignment, the path continuing to be revealed.

I pulled into a humble strip of storefronts in the design district of Dallas, Texas, and saw the sign – Tiger's Den CrossFit – sitting between a sandwich shop and a camera store. I never would have guessed how large and open it was on the inside. At first glance, I wasn't sure what my eyes were seeing. With no weight machines in sight, it definitely wasn't a typical gym. Instead, there was a huge open space from wall to wall and side to side, a warehouse of possibilities. Upon closer study, a playground emerged. In the middle of the open space, lining up from the right wall, five black ropes hung from the ceiling rafters like vines from a tree, beckoning me to climb. Beyond the ropes was a homemade pull-up-bar maze resembling an adult jungle gym, the perimeter of which formed the shape of a square. Near the square were two rows of gymnastics rings suspended from sturdy straps, which led to a line of indoor rowers. Along the front window, a stack of red, yellow, and black square mats resided next to a small mountain of large leather-bound medicine balls. Rows of kettlebells and dumbbells led to a wall of whiteboards. Columns of colorful names and times painted the board. "Workout of the Day" (WOD) was written in big bold letters followed by lines of esoteric code.

On the opposite wall, barbells hung in parallel unison above complementary weightlifting bumper plates, sitting on the floor like stacks of giant color-coded poker chips. Behind them was a section of Olympic lifting platforms. Large tigers played and lounged on the wall in a wood-burned mural – the mark of an artist. Jumbo tractor tires sat lined up in the opposite corner, awaiting their turn. Homemade wooden plyo-boxes were strewn across the open space with more tigers adorning their sides. Educational banners and posters hung on the walls, and a variety of diverse flags waved from the warehouse ceiling.

A peaceful quiet filled the air. Little did I know of all that happens on these sacred grounds. No one was currently pouring the entirety of their being into *the workout*, but I would soon learn first hand how the character of Tiger's Den is fully revealed through engaging in and witnessing a workout. You bond with the surroundings that leave you vulnerable and raw, a safe place to be such, the grounds where you bare your soul through *the challenge*. You bond with the barbells and high bars, rings, and ropes. You bond with the floor as you collapse into it when the clock expires, having pushed and bounded with each foot planted, producing a powerful force of movement with the help of gravity. You bond with "the box" and the field of play beyond it. Transformation happens through *the workout*.

I completed my self-guided tour and rejoined J.D. back at the front counter as he wished farewell to a new athlete. The afternoon sun shone through the front windows. Cars passed on the street beyond the sparse parking lot. We exchanged conversational energy about the gym, life, and everything in between. When asked the popular question, "what else is new?", I alluded to the direction of my life.

"Well, I'm considering taking a leap toward an even more spiritual career path, starting with teaching meditation in some way. Do you all ever do anything like that up here?" I asked.

His reply was immediate.

"You have to help teach a meditation workshop! And you have to meet my friend Scott. We've been talking about offering something like that for our athletes," he exclaimed.

Perhaps J.D., Scott, and I were all waiting for this. It was certainly an interesting turn of events, an unexplored context of teaching despite my personal, yet not fully realized, *meditative fitness* practice. In my previously confirmed intuitions, I only knew I was to teach meditation on a large scale and somehow it would be different. And here we were talking about putting together a meditation program for fitness. "That qualifies as different, all right," I thought.

"How much time do you need?" J.D. asked.

"I don't really need any time," I said, pausing before going all in, "I was a monk in another life." I let it go with a soul-piercing truth and a lighthearted smile. J.D. smiled back, and for a long time, not another word was spoken along those lines, but I always had the sense of a deeper understanding. If I had gone further on that occasion, I might have talked about meditating for a lifetime. I might have talked about meditating in this lifetime, or I might have talked about what precedes, underlies, and trumps it all.

Right then, we saw movement through the front windows and heard the sound of an approaching car. We turned to witness the arrival of an old marked-up truck pulling into the nearest parking space.

"Perfect! Scott's here," said J.D.

We exited the building to greet him properly, where I could see his special truck more clearly. Covering the white paint were spiritual quotes and decorations. On the hood, it read, "There is no way to happiness. Happiness is the way." On the passenger door, it said, "I love you... Yes, you!" On the rear side panel was a cherished poem by Hafiz, called, "How Do I Listen." It emanated the perfect combination of words, "How do I listen to thee, as if everyone were my master, speaking to me his last dying words." The tailgate, painted in large red and gold capital letters, paid homage to "Rumi," another great spiritual poet.

Out hopped Scott, a fairly tall man with short peppered hair, a tan complexion consistent with his Italian heritage, and a genuine radiance for life. His smile was as big as the smiley face painted on the driver's side door. Tattooed on his left arm was an artistic sleeve capped off with another smiley face near his hand. His medium-sized strong and lean frame showed he was fit. A good four inches taller than me, I guessed him to be slightly over six feet tall. J.D. introduced us as we re-entered the Den. With the first mention of the words "meditation," "teaching," and "workshop," Scott lit up, and the energy poured out.

"I would love to help! Fitness helped lead me to spirituality, health, and a new way of life. And meditation has been part of my fitness for a while now..."

All I could do was listen as his passion and enthusiasm flowed, and underneath the words I saw the essence of who he is and his pure heart. We spoke on that first occasion like two similar songs of the soul, dreaming about all the possibilities. Once again, everything, including all the events leading up to then, made sense. We weren't sure how it would all happen, but the three of us could see a grand vision coming into focus. We were to help further and lead a movement that was already taking place. The vision and accompanying intuition was bigger than words could capture. Chills washed over us, and we stood in awe of what was happening.

Two days later, I returned to Tiger's Den for a workout. Scott and I arrived early, and the place was peaceful again. J.D. was waking from his slumber in the attached apartment. Tonka, J.D.'s dog and resident mascot, was ready for his morning relief on the strip of grass out front. Scott opened the large rear warehouse-style doors, letting in a most welcome natural light.

"So, it's a competition called 'Fight Gone Bad'?"

"Sort of, that's the name of *the workout,*" Scott replied.

"Is it as bad as it sounds?" I asked.

"Nah, you got this. All you have to do is as much as you can for three rounds of five minutes, with one minute of rest in between rounds."

"Well, this is it," I thought to myself, "this is what I've been training for. Right here, right now." I was always pretty active, and after training in the gym for years, I felt confident in being able to do okay, maybe even being competitive.

Scott was to guide me through *the workout* and record my score, which would be compared to the other athletes competing later in the day. It was an exciting proposition. I sensed something special taking place. *The workout.* Meditation. Both of us in an empty warehouse, coming together for God and soul purpose, for the benefit of others and the world at large. I practiced calming my nerves and connecting with my breath, preparing my best for what was to come. I swung my legs back and forth and side to side, opening my hips. I arched my back and reached up to the sky to open my chest and align my spine. I swung my arms up and around and across my body, warming my shoulders and stimulating blood flow, preparing my body for movement and exertion. The warm-up was a moving meditation of its own.

Throughout my life, I trained for sports and athleticism. The love first developed in training for high-level tennis, but then later blossomed when I trained for the training itself, the meditative experiences and the moments. I began melding meditation and spiritual practice with my workouts at local gyms, before and after, in between sets, and in the midst of physical exertion. These experiences involved engaging my heart in *the workout*, applying and creating new meditative practices, working with my energy, meditative breathing, and creating inner strength. My workouts served as a consistent spiritual practice. Many parts of this book were inspired by days when I awoke suffering from a kind of spiritual depression. It is no secret that exercise helps release endorphins and combat depression, but what happens when we combine this with conscious meditative focus? I practiced transforming the lower energy and often ended *the workout* in seated meditation. Meditating in an active gym environment is a unique and liberating experience, with others going about their exercises as you send them peace and goodwill. For me personally, it took courage, vulnerability, and surrendering to the perception of others. I remember life-changing moments, leaving the facility running and skipping, pointing to the sky, happy to be alive with a wide-open heart. Coming from the road I once traveled, these moments were nothing short of miracles.

At the same time, I highly valued rigorous physical effort and everything that comes with it. Committed to continuous learning and growing, my *fitness karma* led me to training with variation, functional compound (multiple joint) *movements*, and foundational *lifts*. My body has always had some musculature on a small frame. Weighing in at 142 pounds and standing five feet and seven inches tall, I'd be a featherweight or less for sure. I'm grateful for my small and agile frame and everything it allows me to do. It would be revealed, however, that I was not entirely ready for what was about to take place. Little did I know how much was still to learn as I prepared to be physically introduced to the sport of fitness.

The equipment formed a line in the open space next to the maze of high bars. Near the wall sat a 20-pound medicine ball. A few paces from the wall rested a loaded 75-pound barbell. The weight gave me more confidence. Two more paces and I arrived at a plyo-box. No problem, I thought. Beyond the box sat a rower, which was a foreign object to me despite being found in almost any gym. The proposed workout was 17 minutes long with as much intensity packed into those minutes as individually possible. It seemed simple: a combination of five exercises and *lifts*, scored by total reps, one minute each for three rounds of wall-balls (squatting with a medicine ball, then tossing it up to a target height against the wall), sumo deadlift high pulls (wide sumo stance, narrow grip, standing and pulling the barbell up to your collar bones), box jumps, overhead barbell push presses, and row-ing for calories burned.

After the warm-up and going over the exercises and standards of movement, it was time for *the challenge*. I stood facing the wall holding the 20-pound ball near my chest, one hand placed care-fully on each side so as to provide the best upward thrust. The digital wall timer began to count down in quick but slow passing seconds as my heart beat faster.

"Beep. Beep. Beep. Beeeeeep!" signaled the start with Scott simultaneously yelling, "Go!" in an encouraging tone. In his heart, he knew how special these inaugural moments were.

I started on fire. Standing a foot from the wall, I squatted, rose, and jump-thrusted the ball toward the 10-foot target line. Squat, rise, jump, thrust. Squat, rise, jump, thrust. One after another without stopping. I finished 21 wall balls as furiously as I could in that minute.

"Rotate!" yelled Scott over the music that J.D. had thought-fully cranked on.

Panting heavily, I moved straight to the bar for the sumo deadlift high pulls. I enjoyed this *lift*, exploding off the ground with the bar until it reached a point of weightlessness near my collarbones. One, two, three...on up to 10, 11, 12 before rest was needed for only a moment before going back to work...13, 14, 15, 16. I raced the clock. The concept of pacing was lost on me in those two minutes as I kept going until the short minute was up. In hindsight, long minutes would have been more valuable, and it is all about the way you see the minutes.

"Rotate!" yelled Scott.

I moved on to the box jumps with my heart beating near max capacity and my now hot lungs circulating as much air as possible. No matter, however, I knew I could do some box jumps regardless of how I felt. It's in my spider monkey genes. So I jumped and landed, first on the box, straightening my legs and bouncing lightly on the balls of my feet before falling back to the concrete floor. Jump, land, bounce, fall, jump, land, bounce, fall. Over and over and over. My mind focused on doing as many reps as possible.

I heard "Rotate!" again, indicating it was time to switch to the push press. In an instant, the prior three minutes caught up with me. Pain filled my lungs and body, now burning up on the inside and dripping with sweat. Going from compound *movement* to compound *movement* with no rest was a new experience for me. I gathered myself. Reality descended with only three minutes in and 14 minutes to go. The clock kept ticking. I abandoned the concept of counting in that fourth minute. All mental energy was focused on pressing the barbell overhead in a state of fatigue.

"Rotate!"

Nearly dead after those four minutes, my lungs burned after what felt like the equivalent of sprinting a four-minute mile. Unfamiliar barking and grunting noises came with each exhale. "Asthma attack" flashed through my mind; I couldn't breathe fast enough, which felt like I was drowning. And if I couldn't breathe, I couldn't continue. I managed to lift my arm and hold up my pointer finger to communicate my condition to Scott.

"I can't....breathe....huuhgh....huuhgh....huuhgh," I grunted.

"You are breathing," he said wisely and with more confidence in me than I had in myself at the time.

I stepped dazedly to the rower, sat down, strapped in my feet, and suffered through the row.

"Rest! One minute! Good job, man," said Scott.

I was incapable of speaking, but felt tremendous relief inside. In the brief *rest*, I was still gasping for air, grunting strangely from the middle of my chest with each breath, barely standing. My heart felt constricted yet opening. Then, in that moment, the lights switched fully on. Awareness set in. I was the one exacerbating the hyperventilation. In an instant, I entered a *meditative state,* relaxed my breathing, grounded my energy, and opened my heart. Regathered, I moved to the wall for the next round. *The workout* was the meditation. *The foundation* of my practice had been triggered.

It was here, in minutes six to 17, where the book was born. While doing everything in my power to make it through *the workout,* I saw the connections between meditation and fitness. In a flash, the vision of the book and all the chapters were revealed. Fitness is inherently meditative and contains many elements of meditation. It happened so fast, I could barely grasp it all in those physically intense moments, but I knew immediately it was my duty to write this book.

The rest of *the workout* involved short spurts followed by quick seconds of meditative recovery. Throughout those remaining 11 minutes, I tapped my entire being. I found and relied on *pure intention* to press on and keep moving, a determination to not only continue, but to proceed unstoppable, focused, on a mission. My thoughts aligned, a greater presence was summoned, and awareness made it all possible. While my score was nothing special, I had leaned in to *the challenge* and entered another realm. When Scott finally yelled, "Stop," he put his hand in the air as a validating symbol of the work that was done. I slapped his hand before collapsing to the ground in exhilarated relief.

Within an hour of returning home, I outlined the contents that now make up chapters two through 11: Intention, Presence, Awareness, Thought, Heart, Energy, The Breath, The Body, Food, and Vision. In addition, Scott and I envisioned warm-up, active workout, and recovery meditations. In the coming weeks, these meditations and processes materialized from the moment I awoke to the moment I slept. And when I slept, I dreamt about them. The book took on a life of its own. All throughout my days, I recorded voice memo after voice memo.

These universe-delivered audio recordings comprise the visions and teachings of the book, including the processes as the application and core of this work. There are meditative processes for building *the foundation,* such as anchoring relaxation, connecting with your breath and energy, tuning in to your body, and engaging your heart. Other processes include dedicating your practice, setting intentions for your workouts, rest and recovery meditations, self-hypnotic counting, workout mantras, and more.

As the days turned into weeks, I visited Tiger's Den in addition to my local gym as often as possible. Each workout, each experience, each meditation, each lesson contributed to the book. Elements of the book and practice blossomed as I followed my intuition, conducting experiments and gathering research as the observer of myself and others. Years of meditative workout experiences were coming to fruition.

Meditative fitness is the art of applying meditative elements to your fitness and the movement of your body. It is the spiritual practice of fitness, the inner world of physical exertion, and a method for change and growth in *the four key areas* of heart, mind, body, and soul, creating spiritual integration through fitness. The stories and processes offer practical applications to help you develop your own personal techniques. The purpose of this book is to offer the spiritual engagement along with methods to reach higher performance in any arena. The spiritual and performance aspects walk hand-in-hand. With the help of specific meditation principles, you can hone your natural abilities, access untapped potential, break through barriers, shatter limiting beliefs, and take flight in your practice.

Meditative fitness as outlined here is a combination of sitting, standing, and moving meditation. The techniques are not limited to *the workout,* but rather extend to your life at large. Once you have established a foundation, you can alter the energy of your body with a single breath. You can relax and enter a *meditative state* with ease. Breath by breath, you build your practice.

The practice is yours and about you, personal and unique in nature. More than anything, it is about what is real and true to you and what you want. The choices of how and what to do with it are yours, and you may apply this text in any way you choose. This is your life. Anything happening in your life and the way you feel serves as an inner reflection and is part of your practice. Everything that surfaces from within is an opportunity for growth. You can choose to deal with things that haven't been given a voice, life experiences, thoughts, feelings, and energy – the life under the surface. Your practice is your creation in alignment with your faith. You build it and make it your own, starting with your first meditation, your next meditation, or your next meditative workout.

My hope is that this book will inspire the engagement of your workouts and lead to overwhelming health. The days of exercising for vain and shallow reasons are over. Higher consciousness and depth of heart await. No longer the resistance, *the workout* is no longer a chore. You no longer need to suffer to get through a workout. Expand the realm of possibilities. Expand your reasons for engaging in your workouts. It is time to surrender and embrace, align with true strength, and dedicate your workouts to greater meaning and higher purpose.

The text in this book provides such guidance as the culmination of lifetimes and influence of many spiritual masters, teachers, and practices that have come before. Yoga paves the way; *Meditative Fitness* broadens the horizon. Physical yoga, a series of asanas or yoga postures, as commonly practiced, represents only one of the eight arms of yoga. In relation to *the practice* described in these pages, physical yoga could be part of *the practice* or none of *the practice*. Less commonly known, the asanas are meant to serve as a meditation and help prepare one for meditation. Meditative yoga and the other seven arms are connected to all that we do. My hope is that this book will help deepen a yoga practice as well as offer a blissful alternative.

The practice is defined here as: *1.)* A *meditative fitness* practice, including your physical practice and journey of growth – *the workout,* meditation, mobility work, nutrition, and any other fitness or spiritual work. *2.)* Ongoing in nature, a way of engaging life from a place of learning, observing your inner world, open for self-realization – applying meditative and spiritual principles for the purpose of happiness, awakening, and enlightening. *3.)* Working toward mastery in any area of your life.

Welcome to the world of *meditative fitness.* In some ways this is a revolutionary concept for the fitness world. In other ways this is a revolutionary concept of a spiritual practice. At the same time, it isn't revolutionary at all, for the simple truth that it's already happening.

In physical exertion, which we refer to as *the workout,* meditative phenomena happen readily. Inner growth happens as a result of overcoming physical challenges. These are not new concepts, but new awarenesses, connections, and correlations. Each chapter addresses an element to help create your practice and better engage a meditative workout. At the end of chapters are processes for reference. Feel free to read or complete them at any time. As perhaps the most valuable part of this work, they provide the framework, application, and deeper understanding of the text. If you were to only go through the processes, you would gain a personal grasp of the concepts in the book. The combination of both, however, will prove most empowering. Throughout these pages, you will see the vast connections. Perhaps some will be a joyous reminder of what you already know, while others will shed new light as a process of expanding awareness.

Yes, you will learn how to meditate. Yes, you already know how to meditate. Close your eyes and focus on your breath, and you may begin. Does this mean you have to meditate? No. Does this mean you have to change anything you are currently doing? No. You will benefit simply by reading these concepts, and you can easily apply them to your everyday life and fitness experiences. If, however, you choose to have a sitting practice, you will see areas of your life and fitness rise to new levels.

To reach your full potential in fitness arenas and be happier while doing it, to transform your workouts into a purpose-driven opportunity for growth, all you have to do is establish *the foundation*, do the groundwork, and create your practice with any amount of meditation. Five, 10, 15, or 20 minutes is enough to work miracles. Longer periods and multiple times a day are a beautiful bonus. A single step is all it takes to start a journey. Set aside specific times and follow through on the commitment. *The practice* maximizes your time in your workouts and overflows into all areas of your life. The results are eye-opening and enlightening.

You are the master of your inner world guided by your inner wisdom. Mastery begins by taking ownership of your inner world and outer reactions, which can make the difference between feeling sane or insane. The subconscious and depths of emotion ascend as the tip of the iceberg, surface-level being. You are responsible for what you are creating for yourself, the way you think, feel, and act. So often we look outside of ourselves for ways to improve our lives when it really starts on the inside. This is much more vast than relying solely on self, but the connection happens within. Each of us has the ability to tune in to our truth, an intuitive knowing. You are the one with your answers in relation to your spiritual life.

What kind of person do you want to be?

In life? In your interactions with others?

What is important to you?

What are you devoted to?

How do you feel about your health and fitness?

Are you passionate, energized, happy, and alive?

Or overwhelmed, embarrassed, lethargic, and depressed?

Start from where you are and move from there.

It is time to be honest with yourself.

It is time to engage *the practice*.

Meditation is a technology of heart, mind, and body, a technology of spirit and the soul. For beginners, learning how to meditate is like learning a new computer program. Sometimes you just have to get in there and start clicking until you find your way. Remove judgments of good and bad; there is no right or wrong way to meditate. Any meditation (or physical exercise) is better than none. There is only the way it is, the way you do it, and allowing the results to speak. From here, there are many depths, layers, and levels of mastery. It can be beneficial to practice a variety of skills and techniques. There are infinite things you can do in your inner world, or you may *go in* and do nothing at all – the baseline of relaxing and being with your breath is always there.

Meditation is a state of being: calm your mind and body; access a deeper state and a higher form of intelligence; engage your heart; slow your brainwaves to a relaxed, yet alert and focused place of *pure intention.* There is passive meditation and active meditation. The perfect union and complement of both can be most beneficial. Passive meditation includes relaxation, letting all else go for a moment, spending time with your breath, spending time with God, aligning and listening for what the Universe has for you. Active meditation is when we are actively doing things such as clearing our energy, visualizing, opening our hearts and releasing underlying emotion, chanting, repeating an affirmation, or moving *the body.* Meditation is a space to see and imagine, to feel things otherwise not felt, and to create our lives and the way we engage them.

As soon as you close your eyes, your brainwaves begin to slow down. Your senses heighten as you turn inward while more aware of the external world. Your imagination has cause and empowerment over that which you focus your intention. Meditation is a space of healing and working with the metaphysical in relation to your body, the world of the unseen: thoughts, heart, energy, and spirit. The gambit can be overwhelming, but is quickly dispelled by the simple act of breathing.

Close your eyes and start to feel the air that fills your lungs, the life and energy that animates your body. Close your eyes and learn how to see without them. Realize your most natural and eternal state of being, who you are and will always be. This is what it feels like to be alive. This is where you become the master.

Through meditation, be yourself, all that you are, and enter a universe of knowledge within. Work with your subconscious; program the computer; rewire circuits; tune in at the cellular level; tap into your nervous system; and promote the natural flow of your body's intricate workings. All this, you do with practice. You *go in* and allow small miracles to manifest, realize abilities, and test what you are capable of. You *go in,* follow the meditation, and see where it leads. You try something new and surprise yourself in amazement. A special kind of genius takes place within.

All of life is a meditation. Your state of being is always happening. The question is, what type of meditation would you like it to be? How would you like to engage your life and the world around you? Meditation is an empowering state where all it takes is a moment to rise in vibration to a happier, more joyous, loving, and aware existence. The more formal sitting meditation helps you connect with your most natural state of being, whereupon you open your eyes to the real you and welcome yourself home. No matter where you go, you can go home within yourself. This is where you live, right where you are at the center of being. Most of all, meditation is something you experience and discover for yourself. To continue your journey, go to the processes at the end of the book, start the exploration, and prepare for *the workout.*

Processes for Reference

The Workout

"Here I am," I say to myself with butterflies in my stomach as I pull in next to Scott's spirit-truck. Inner processing heightens at the thought of what my second workout might hold. The sun, an hour above the horizon, marks a new day, with Tiger's Den awakening as well. Walking through the doors reminds me of entering a sanctuary, a place to give yourself to something greater, a place with deeper meaning, where bonds are formed through heart, purpose, and sweat. *The workout* is now a sacred time, the work a sacred engagement. I arrive with a sense of gratitude. A new chapter has begun. Each person I pass receives my ongoing subconscious prayer, wanting all to be happy and fulfilled. When I reach the heart of the Den, I pause with a deep breath and gather my energy, bringing it down within my body before breathing back up within myself. Aligned and present, my intention is set, knowing what I do is for the benefit of all.

J.D. is busy hanging a educational banner. He moves on to arrange some of the adult playground equipment, constantly improving this special place endearingly known as the Den. I join Scott in front of the wall of whiteboards.

He welcomes me with a joyful "Yo!" and extends his hand for a half-shake, half-hug. "You ready for a 'meditative wod?'"

"I sure am," I smile, "what is it?"

"Ah yeah! You're gonna like this one, and we can do it together."

The handwritten workout stares at us from the whiteboard and provides a mirror to the thoughts and feelings that arise as a result. This time, *the challenge* is dauntingly obvious. Regardless of conditioning, and perhaps by some Divine intervention, this workout (in addition to my first one at the Den) is a monumental challenge for the benefit of things to come.

"It's called 'Glenn,' named for a fallen soldier," says Scott.

In silence we allow that statement to sink in. With reverence, *the workout* is dedicated to something greater than ourselves. This "hero" wod involves 30 clean and jerks (cleaning the barbell from the ground to your shoulders, then dipping and driving it overhead, ending in a stable, standing overhead position) followed by a one-mile run. Upon your return, climb the beckoning 15-foot rope to the rafters a total of 10 times. Then, run another mile followed by 100 burpees. The goal is to complete these tasks in the least amount of time, checking the clock upon your finish so you can proudly write that number on the whiteboard.

Other than the running, which I haven't done much of in ages, these are all new exercises for me. As insurmountable as it seems, I look forward to this. I know it will hurt, but somewhere in there, I also know the rewards will be well worth this kind of hurt. I must find more strength than I otherwise possess. It will test all of me, providing the perfect opportunity for growth and a meditative workout.

In physical exertion, we build strength, exercise agility, and develop mobility and movement patterns. We test ourselves and learn what we are capable of. We grow and measure our growth, and we have fun moving *the body*. We inspire and get inspired by others, and we intimately share in the vulnerability of our level of fitness. Through physical exertion, we exercise what it means to be human.

The workout is defined here as: *1.)* Any form of physical exertion. *2.)* A series of *skills, lifts,* and *movements,* including strength training, skill work, and cardio or metcons (metabolic conditioning). i.e., part of a fitness regimen: CrossFit, weightlifting, yoga, spin, attending group classes, going to your local gym, cycling, running, walking, dancing, or playing sports. *3.)* As part of a *meditative fitness* practice, *the workout* is the meditation.

"Can you remember the first time you meditated at the gym?" I ask.

Scott responds with a wide grin, "It was in an aerobics room. I sat quietly on a yoga mat in the corner. I remember closing my eyes and gathering all the energy I could, sending it to everyone in the gym, then extending it to all beings. I sent my strength out into the Universe and asked in return to borrow whatever I needed to get through my workout. And I sat quietly focusing on breathing in and out.

"*The workout* flowed effortlessly from there. I didn't have to think about what I wanted to do or the weights I was going to use. It came instinctively as if predetermined, like an out-of-body experience. There was a sense of connectedness with everyone and everything around me. As the experience grew, so did strength. I ended it back in the aerobics room with my eyes closed, calming down, and breathing. And when I opened my eyes, I saw beauty everywhere."

I know exactly what he means, having had similar yet uniquely personal experiences over the years. If you want to create a more meditative workout, it can be as simple as a few calming breaths, a sincere moment, or a couple of minutes of warm-up meditation prior to movement. It can be as simple as some meditative breaths throughout *the workout* or a couple of minutes of recovery meditation afterwards. If this is all you read and all you do, then it is a good starting point for your practice. From here, however, there is much to expand on.

The workout interrupts patterns of thought and behavior and can help quiet an overactive mind in the same manner as physical yoga, chanting, or the repeating of mantras and affirmations. Meditative in nature, *the workout* serves as a form of processing to help rewire and reprogram. Infinite possibilities abound for practicing the art of *meditative fitness,* each workout a unique experience and expression.

A meditative workout can include gathering strength before *lifts*, repeating a positive thought while completing repetitions, and flowing from *movement* to *movement.* Or it may include a series of *rest period* meditations, followed by meditative mobility and a post-workout sitting practice. One of the greatest benefits of meditating post-workout is calming your nervous system after it has been revved up. Meditation helps with recovery much like sleep does. Fifteen minutes of deep meditation is said to be the equivalent of three hours of sleep. Like lying in savasana at the end of a yoga class, even two to five minutes can help calm your nervous system.

All it requires at the beginning of *the workout* is a deep, slow, attentive breath or series of breaths. With practice and the development of neural connections, you can enter a *meditative state* with ease. Once entered, you can come out of it and return to it readily as you flow through your workouts. As you execute any series or sets of repetitions, you can enter a transcendent state of being.

Scott and I continue our warm-up by practicing the clean and jerk with an empty barbell. J.D. provides instruction and acts as an external set of eyes, focusing on our positions. I focus on the feeling of the *lift*. You can feel it when it happens just right – the inner knowing. The *movement* feels more effortless, the weight feels lighter, recruiting the primary muscles for the job, aided by *the breath* at just the right time, coming from a place of inner and outer strength. I trust and rely on this inner knowing in relation to *lifts* and life.

While setting off on the lifelong journey of mastering this *lift*, I practice going into an ideal state to enter *the workout*.* I am present and still aware of the circulating nerves. With my eyes open, I settle inward, connect with intention, and relax. I glance over at Scott, who appears to be doing the same. Neither of us could know for sure without asking, for a meditative workout can take place right next to you with or without your knowing. Many times I have done this in the gym, seated at the end of a bench or standing still for a meditative moment. A sensitive eye is required to notice subtle shifts in others, rather than being too absorbed in our own little worlds.

Our warm-up ends, but *the practice* is only beginning. The clock counts down from 10 to zero with a long "beeeep" signaling the start. Forty-seven minutes later, *the workout* ended for Scott. Twenty grueling minutes after that, it ended for me; but the sheer fact that I completed the tasks is the more remarkable truth. This workout was a deep meditation. In between the beeping start and the eventual expended collapse on the floor is where incredible things happen.

A meditative workout is a time for setting intentions based on your current state. Too often we engage life, circumstances, food, and exercise from a place of resistance. Before, during, or after *the workout* is the perfect time to say a little prayer, ask and allow, surrender, and connect to your truth. As a physical meditation, *the workout* sparks change and life within. It wakes and liberates aspects of who you are. It helps open your heart, activate energy centers, and create pathways. It impacts the cellular level of your body. *The workout* serves as a defibrillator, shocking slumbering cells to life. Flatline no more, *the workout* lets you know you are alive. You are only ever one workout away from awakening and feeling good. One meditative experience can change the course of your life and the way you engage it, potentially changing every moment of every day. You may come to a time where everything you do contributes to the meditation, to *the workout,* and to your growth as you prostrate yourself in *the challenge.* To be consistent in your practice, always know when your next workout will be. You are only ever one workout away.

Scott finished first in hoisting the clean and jerks and started running his mile, leaving a lasting impression. I felt left behind watching his silhouette recede, framed by the warehouse doors, while I pushed through the reps. A couple of minutes later, after my 30th overhead barbell victory stance, I jogged toward the rear cargo doors, jumped down the three-foot drop to the concrete, and ran with my arms hanging at my sides, shaking them out. Collin, one of the coaches, ran with me for a bit to encourage me as well as show me the way. We made a slight right down an alley leading to an adjoining side street, where he dropped off. I found myself striding down the middle of the street in the industrial design district. After another curve, I caught a glimpse of Scott leading the way. With a surge of joy, the chase was on. There is no doubt that going through this with him changed *the workout* and experience for me. Scott's presence inspired me to keep going and lean in to *the challenge*.

As I ran, I practiced becoming lighter physically and in spirit. I adopted the most efficient movement, gliding with each touch of the ground, the weight of life lifting and dispersing with the calm breeze. I imagined running in the clouds and felt as though I was floating across the pavement.

When I returned to the box, Scott was tapping the rusty ceiling rafters for his second or third rope ascent. I didn't realize how hard the rope climbs would be after the clean and jerks and the first mile run. Both of us reached a wall – our arms were spent. Neither of us knew how to use our legs on the rope. Collin came over and demonstrated a useful foot technique, which we didn't have time to master with the clock still ticking, adding to surfacing stress and frustration. We were challenged in more ways than physical. Fear and doubt arose from within. I questioned whether we were going to be able to do them all.

After each climb, the question grew louder. Rests between ascents became longer as we recovered strength. Heart was engaged through the fears and doubts, which were replaced by determination. The last three ascensions called for absolutely everything we could muster. Energy flows in accordance with strength of will for the pure of heart – the greater the will, the greater the energy. We willed our way to the top 10 times. In fact, I made it 10.9 times due to my second-to-last attempt. Nearly to the top, the rafters a half-foot away, I had nothing left. If I only knew how to use my legs, I could have rested a moment. My arms pulled up and my body went nowhere. I could barely continue to hold on. I had truly reached my physical limit in that attempt, but the task was not complete. I retreated safely back to earth, rested in a *meditative state*, gathered energy, recharged, and eyed the rope with *pure intention*. Nothing was going to stop me from reaching the rafters. I bee-lined to the top with all the strength I had in me, calling on the Universe to help me. With my muscles near failure, carefully holding on with one arm, the rope braced between my legs, I reached up to touch the rafters. Success! Never had I been so happy to go run a mile. If only the mile was the finish; the grand finale, 100 burpees, proved to be the most sneaky gut-wrenching adversary. A burpee is basically going from standing, down to a pushup, followed by a jumping overhead clap; five to 10 are enough to get a little winded. Five burpees. Rest. Five burpees. Rest. In each rest I composed myself. I stepped outside a couple of times for fear of losing the contents of my stomach. It became about finishing, and I understood why I had to finish, how it symbolized so much more. I had to rise to *the challenge.* Five burpees. Rest. All the way to 100, one crawling burpee at a time. The finish line was in sight with peace waiting on the other side.

As an important element of life and *the workout*, *the challenge* represents a level of difficulty unique to the individual, a test of ability, outside of one's comfort zone. *The challenge* leads to wisdom, adaptation, and growth. Physical challenges lead to the mental, emotional, and spiritual side of the equation, sparking thoughts, emotion, and other aspects of your inner world to move through in your practice.

Rising to greater heights depends on whether you answer *the call*, an inner summoning, intuition, or whisper from within to rise to *the challenge*, live in your truth, and face the path that lies before you. Life is a continuous offering of whether to answer *the call*.

There are ongoing prayers in your soul.

Are you answering *the call?*

Will you allow God/the Universe/inner wisdom to guide you?

Will you expand your perceived limitations?

Will you answer *the call* of *the workout?*

How often do you hold back?

How much of you is hidden,

waiting to awaken through *the challenge*?

We can choose to ignore *the call* and lead mediocre lives, or lives of depression and anxiety, dependent on medication to at the very least not be miserable. Or we can answer *the call*, rise and discover our potential, and be more fulfilled than we ever imagined, overcoming any adversity placed before us. Choosing this path of the spiritual warrior leads to a lifetime of wisdom and growth. In this way, there is no victim of life and life's circumstances, only blessings and gifts, awakening through *the challenge.*

What challenges you in life, and how do you challenge yourself? Look closely. What will you transform, and what gifts will you realize?

You are the only one who can hold yourself back in relation to what challenges you. Life calls for us to dance in front of a great number of onlookers. Imagine stepping onstage, untrained, wanting to dance your best dance. You know that your only chance is to allow yourself to move freely rather than restrained, to find something greater within. With no training to rely on, you have to trust yourself. No more holding back being locked up. You let go and allow yourself to be the real and authentic you, all of you, a most precious being, dancing in the moment.

A meditative workout is a dance with the Divine. *The challenge* determines the nature of the dance and can lead to greater heart and presence, strength of intention, and further awakening. Challenges help us to be humble and vulnerable, which are essential qualities for growth as well as connection and intimacy with others. When we go through challenges together, we bond through the shared experience.

A physical challenge can be long or short in duration. One can easily create a significant challenge by repeating any functional *movement.* For another simple formula, choose any two or three *lifts* or *movements*, and alternate (with a particular rep scheme) until you must rest. The trick is to enjoy all of it. From now on, hard equals fun. Applying this simple notion transforms your experience. The harder it is, the more fun you are having. One mantra to repeat when it gets hard in *the workout* is, "We're having fun now," with a smile. And if you need to let out a primal grunt or a playful "Wooh!" then go ahead and do that too.

When we don't push ourselves, or when we don't embrace the physical exertion, we run the risk of fooling and cheating ourselves. We must be honest regarding how much we want what we say we want. How much effort are you willing to give? Where do you set the bar? Do you go through the motions or engage with healthy passion and energy? Are you negative and complaining, or do you remain positive? Will you take action and allow yourself to be happy and fulfilled?

Often when embarking on a new path of growth or change, when we tell ourselves we're going to "get in shape" or "get healthy," all kinds of thoughts, feelings, and behavior patterns rise to the surface. Do not be surprised if your inner world is shaken up, revealing aspects of yourself to clear and move through toward something better. On the path of growth, this is the opportunity when life stirs things up and presses your buttons, the same opportunity in meditation and *the workout*.

You may find yourself feeling down if you struggle to make it to the gym. Use this as motivation rather than self-sabotage. It is all a valuable part of *the practice*. You can expect inner barriers to reveal themselves; embrace them, for they provide the possibility for healing and quantum level growth. Face a barrier and strengthen in will and spirit. Get knocked down. Get back up. Don't want to get back up? Too bad, get back up anyway. Get knocked down again. Get back up with *pure intention* and determination. This is the opportunity of *the challenge,* and it arrives in many forms.

It is time to align, time for all things to line up for a common purpose. Your job is to inwardly match your vibration with that of wellness.

The game is simple.

How good can you feel?

How healthy and clear can you be?

The practice helps you align with true strength – honest, humble, and vulnerable, an inner surrender with genuine courage. True strength comes from within and is balanced in *the four key areas.* With emotional strength, stand secure no matter what you may feel, willing to feel all of it without adverse reactions. With mental strength, thoughts are in alignment, providing further fuel and energy. With physical strength, *the body* is your fortress. With spiritual strength, find peace and overcome any challenge, free to be you and to love and care about others. True strength is inner calm in a time of turmoil, gratitude in a time of struggle, and lovingkindness in a time of hate – a shining light in the darkness. True strength is peace in the intensity of physical exertion.

May *the workout* and all food, water, sleep, thoughts, feelings, and energy align with who you are and your heart's pure desire, helping you to feel so good that even if you slip, it doesn't matter. It is your way of life, and a detour doesn't change this. Even it serves a purpose. Find the value in the detour and you find yourself on the path.

Amid everything else, you can have fun. *The workout* isn't meant to be a chore, something you "have" to do. You can laugh through your workouts. You can liberate yourself through dance or meditation when no one else is dancing or meditating. Confront fears of how others may perceive you, let go of self-image, and let yourself be happy. Earth is perhaps the greatest playground, obstacle course, and arena in existence. Everywhere you go, you may engage in *the workout.* Walk. Step. Run. Jump. Leap. Bound. Dance. Climb. Push. Pull. Carry. Press. Squat. Lunge. A great many things can be done for a workout. Doesn't it feel good to move your body? Enjoy every moment and every *movement.* Embrace your surroundings and complement your environment with your presence.

After Scott and I finished *the workout,* in a state of shock, it was as though my body didn't know what had happened. We actively relaxed and recovered while working on tight areas. After some mobility work, we walked across the box, out the rear doors, down the cargo lot and alley, until we circled back at the front again.

"How do you feel?" I asked as we stepped through the open door.

"Fantastic, how about you, wanna do it again?" joked Scott.

"Ha-hm-hm," I coughed with the remnants of discomfort in my lungs.

We sat down on the black rubber flooring in the middle of the open space. We stretched some more until we were both sitting in a meditative posture. Sitting and breathing, we talked peacefully about what had taken place and the meditative qualities therein. Surely endorphins had been released, contributing to the pleasantness in our expressions. Surely our central nervous systems had been tested. There was a sense of release and accomplishment.

"It feels like my energy's been cleared, like every cell has been turned on. No heaviness. Instead, it's like this light buzzing sensation, must be left over from all that cellular friction," I said.

"I know what you mean, hard to put into words," said Scott.

"You know how meditating with even one other person magnifies the energy, I'd say that definitely applies to fitness too. It made a huge difference going through that together," I said.

"Glenn," Scott said in awe.

"Yeah. Glenn," I said in understanding. Glenn now held a special place in our hearts. We will forever remember that workout, that day, that experience. We will forever be grateful for Glenn.

Processes for Reference

2

Intention

————— ◎ —————

I LOOKED UP and stared down the gymnastics rings, as if to say, "I mean this, rings." I was ready to attempt my first muscle-up. No guarantees, but I believed I could do it, and I was determined to levitate myself up there. I jumped and adjusted into the best false grip I could muster. Time was of the essence as I swung my legs forward, then backward, and forward again until I sensed the perfect moment to explosively pull and fly through the air. Instinctively, I rolled to catch myself with the rings securely under my shoulders. A split second after realizing what happened, I locked out my arms to complete the *movement.*

"Sweet! First try?!" J.D. yelled. "How'd you do it, visualization?"

"Similar," I replied, "it was *pure intention.*"

In between my newfound physical meditations at the Den, I paid visits to my local gym. These private journeys through *the workout* were where my practice began, and they have always provided much soulful enjoyment. After the eye-opening encounters at Tiger's Den and the birth of this book, it was clear no workout would be the same. There was no going back. My *fitness karma* had changed. Paradigms had shifted, and intention was heightened. Greater was the focused effort in engaging *the challenge,* and there was new life in *the practice.* I began training for future experiences at the Den, practicing new *skills, lifts,* and *movements.* Fitness has *movements* to master like yoga has postures to master, which require practice, patience, and progression. They challenge us mentally, emotionally, and physically. Taken further, mastery of elements in fitness and yoga both call for increased mobility – opening joints, expanding ranges of motion, and training *the body* to reach positions and move freely.

As I navigated through my enlightening workouts, I focused on capturing the essence of intention. In my first workout at Tiger's Den, intention played a key role and illuminated the similarities between meditation and fitness. When my lungs gave out and my body pleaded with me to stop, intention kept me going. It was simple and empowering, the resilient intention to continue despite adversity. Meditative intention calmed and relaxed my breathing, and heart-level resolve arose all the way to the time-ticking finish line.

Meditative fitness is intention, focusing your will with purpose in every *movement. The practice* begins with your intention, each workout an opportunity in time. Embodying intention is core to the state of being found in *meditative fitness.* It makes the difference between a normal workout and a meditative workout. Intention creates purpose, sparks the heart, fans passion, and spurs growth.

Fitness is a spiritual practice when you make it a spiritual practice. Setting your intention is the first step, making it conscious. As soon as you declare within yourself, "Fitness is part of my spiritual practice," the wheels are set in motion. As soon as your practice is dedicated, it changes and begins anew. Intention determines what your practice will become for you. You make it what it is. The layers include your highest intentions, intentions for your practice, your workouts, and meditative, *pure intention*. We will open the doors and examine this mystical world of intention.

Another way to think of intention is not thought, but that which overrides thought, coming from deeper within, a stronger form of consciousness. The goal is for thoughts to align with intention. We wouldn't make it to our workouts without first having the thought or intention to do so. Weak or false intention is the same as lacking commitment, which also applies to executing *skills, lifts,* and *movements.* We aren't going to move a heavy weight or physically push and exert ourselves without a strong intention to do so. However, it is possible to engage *the workout* with very little intention of doing anything significant, physically or otherwise.

Some thoughts come up that we have no intention of fulfilling. Other thoughts come up that we fully intend to act on and carry through. Then there are some thoughts we are absolutely certain will come to fruition; they are connected to a *pure intention*, resonating with heart and truth, as if already in motion. This is found in the execution of meditative intention, and whether we realize it, intention is always with us as a living prayer, an ongoing self-fulfilling prophecy, creating our results in life and our actions that speak louder than our thoughts and words.

Our actions reveal the strength of our true intention. With this engagement, there are no excuses, only the choices we make. Wave goodbye to fooling yourself in denial. Honesty is required to grow. Purity of intention determines the results, and thus you may need to address counter-intentions. The stronger of the two determines which one wins. Counter-intentions are how you sabotage yourself. You can prevent your intention from being realized by not believing it is possible, not believing in yourself, or having some other subconscious block. Once recognized, doubts and limiting beliefs can be overridden by higher intentions. Ongoing in nature, intention can also be reset at any time.

Creating meditative *pure intention* is a self-realized skill. Once developed in your practice, it will carry over into other areas of your life. Some life-altering experiences with *pure intention* will always stay with you. For example, I remember sitting in my friend Frank's Cadillac as we departed Tampa on our way to Dallas. The night before, I had eaten and slept poorly. I woke up groggy and walked around in a fog of tired energy as we prepared for a 17-hour drive. Tired wasn't an option, yet I felt sick I was so tired; I didn't even think sleep would help. Sitting in the spacious passenger seat while Frank took the first shift, I had the inclination to find out what was possible.

"I'm going to meditate and see if I can wake up," I said as the car sped down the road. I put the seatback in a vertical position to help straighten my spine. I pulled my legs up to sit cross-legged in the cozy space, closed my eyes, and tuned in. Sitting in meditation as the vehicle soared down the highway at 80 miles an hour provided a unique floating sensation. Held up by the seat, I hovered a few feet above the pavement. I felt the vibration of the moving vehicle and heard the wind singing against the windows.

Allowing intention to be the prayer, I imagined a protective bubble around us as we traveled through time and space. I took deep powerful breaths in and out, inhaling as much oxygen as possible with the intention of flooding and clearing. I imagined the incoming oxygen as awake energy emanating from the center of my spine, expelling the fog from within. Before long, I felt the buzzing sensation that comes with this type of breathing, and I applied the vibration to clearing out the tired energy.

With each inhale, I moved on to gathering the toxic energy. With each exhale, I let it go, imagining it leaving through my pores and energy field. I felt a connection among my gut, chest, throat, and head. As each breath reached the top of my lungs, yawns were triggered in correlation to the tired energy collecting. The exhales became slow yawns. Different than normal, they were powerful and releasing. My eyes began to water as I followed the meditation down this path. With each breath, I became the *pure intention* of clearing energy. My face contorted and scrunched on the exhales as tired molecules departed, a strange sensation like toxicity leaving my body. Drop by drop, tears fell from my watery eyes, streaming down my cheeks and chin, dripping onto my clothes below. I wiped my cheeks only to have them drenched again seconds later. My sinuses cleared and my nose ran as the intention-filled yawns continued until the cloudy, heavy energy could no longer be felt. No more yawns, only a strong and awake presence of peace. Remaining in a space of *pure intention,* I continued to breathe clear and awake energy for a few minutes, touching every cell. Still floating down the road at high speed, I felt as weightless as the protective bubble surrounding us, and when I was ready, I opened my eyes with a huge smile on my face.

"Whoa! I've never felt more awake in my life!" I exclaimed in near disbelief. "And 15 minutes ago I was ready to pass out. This is crazy."

"Awesome! I feel more awake just sitting next to you." said Frank.

I remained wide awake for the rest of the journey into the late night and early morning hours. Since that day, I have practiced this oxygen flood release* many times.

I had a similar experience releasing knots at the gym after a workout. For weeks I felt them clumped in the muscles between my neck and right shoulder blade. I closed my eyes, went inside, flooded *the body* with oxygen, and moved the vibration to the area. I breathed from the space of the knots, tapped into my central nervous system, and sent oxygen and energy. I went into the knots as *pure intention* and felt them miraculously disperse with a burst of warmth all at once. A small miracle, the knots that had been plaguing me for weeks were gone.

The essence of *pure intention* is faith in action, an absolute belief, focus, and expectation. Aligning with *pure intention* creates magnetism with all energy flowing the same direction. We attract where our intention is placed. *Pure intention* is not forceful, but a fulfilling truth. It is knowing an outcome, knowing that if you want to clear your field of energy, then you may do so, and it is going to happen. *Pure intention* leads the way and everything else follows. It is a determination and will that moves your body, moves the weights, and propels you through *the workout*. With it comes a commitment to the execution.

How will you use *pure intention*?

How will you step closer to your highest good?

The intention of *Meditative Fitness* is to help us move toward our highest potential as athletes and human beings. Whether you are interested in reaching higher performance and conditioning, breaking personal records, hitting milestones in your life, creating a healthy body, weighing your ideal weight, or simply enjoying your practice, intention leads the way. Regardless of the type of physical exertion, *meditative fitness* takes flight with the intention behind *the practice* and movement of your body. Allowing yourself to be humble and vulnerable, let your highest self answer the following questions:

For what reasons do you exercise?

What motivates you to get moving?

What is the intention behind your practice?

What is your intention in reading this?

What outcomes would you like?

And what do they mean to you?

What actions will you take?

What commitments will you make right now?

Meditative Fitness may change your answers to these questions as you connect with your higher self and alternatives to shallow motivations. Personally, I exercise because I am committed to being happy and taking care of myself. Part of me moves my body as a spiritual practice. Part of me does it for my mental and physical health. Part of me does it because I love to move my body, because I see athletic movement as similar to dance. I do it because it feels good to do something physical and release energy, because I love to sweat. I love the way it feels afterward, love when my legs feel strong, and love knowing that I worked hard. Part of me moves my body as an act of love toward myself. Part of me does it for the way my body looks and feels as a result. When practicing *meditative fitness*, all layers serve the same highest intention. No part better or worse than another, there is no judgment of the parts. The whole is who you are.

Each workout is a test or measure of your intention and can serve to strengthen intention. The result of how you feel provides the feedback. By only going through the motions, we don't find many results, and we don't feel as good about our effort. No one finishes a marathon without the strong intention to do so. Even in reading this right now, you can either be going through the motions or connecting with intention. *The workout* along with meditation serves as intention muscle-building with small successes adding up to exponential change.

In an intense workout, you quickly begin to feel everything that comes with maximum exertion. Your muscles fill with lactic acid. Your lungs take in as much air as possible, and the overall sensation engulfs your body. When this happens, notice your inner dialogue as you survey your body in motion. Will you talk yourself into stopping or will you allow your intention to override?

When you think you can't continue, and when your body pleads with you to stop, pure heart-level resolve takes over.

This is the unique opportunity that limit-pushing physical effort offers daily through *the workout*. In those moments when your fitness is tested, you rely on intention to keep going and summon great heart to go along for the ride. You find more within yourself. You access something inside that propels you forward. Much like holding a demanding pose in yoga or gymnastics, when you're not sure how long you can hold on, yet all you have is the will to do so. The key is to do this from a place of surrender rather than resistance, uniting with the sensations rather than fighting against them. Your mind and body may tell you they want to stop, but strength of will overrides as you reach these false limits and push through them. This is a form of inner strength to align with in your workouts.

Quieting your mind in meditation often involves focus and repetition, such as following your breath or repeating a mantra. Focusing your mind helps quiet your mind, quieting the chatter that can often fill it. Focus and repetition in *the workout* can help in the same manner. When you focus your entire being on the task at hand, when you are focused only on counting your repetitions, the rest of your mind goes quiet. You are no longer worrying about the future or thinking about problems, your to-do list, or the overwhelm of life. This peace of mind can be part of your daily practice. A quiet mind is ideal for setting deeper and higher intentions for yourself and your life. Enjoy the journey as you observe your health and fitness reach new heights. Soon you will be making new goals with results happening with ease.

Meditation is a perfect companion for *the workout.* Whether consciously or not, athletes have been meditating since the beginning of sport, putting themselves in an ideal state to perform. An athlete's intention determines results. How often have we seen a particular game where one team has more will and energy than the other? As a result, the law of attraction is on their side, and everything seems to go their way. The team with the greater collective intention generally wins the battle. And when two teams have an equally high degree of intention, it may be a classic in the making, a game to be remembered, with cosmic chance, grace, or a slight physical advantage rising above the other.

Meditative intention is found in the execution. As in the example of clearing tired energy, you become the intention, and you flow from one intention to another within broader intentions. Developing meditative intention is highly valuable to incorporate in your workouts. Imagine being really tuned in with heightened senses, putting yourself in a calm, yet purely focused state, with an unbreakable will. Imagine gathering all of your strength before *lifts*, visualizing your *movement*, creating a positive flow of energy, and relaxing your heart rate and breathing when needed. There are infinite intentions to embody. You write the pattern. The formula is simple. *Go in* and set your intention at a deeper state of mind, then let it go, and repeat. May your highest intentions lead the way.

Intention allows us to flow between active and passive meditation. This can look like chanting followed by moments of silence, physical yoga or *the workout* followed by sitting meditation, and so on. In passive meditation, with the intention of simply being, you can connect with the life within you and all around. Thoughts appear and fade away as you realize you are so much more. This is the place where you allow yourself to simply be... surrendering, listening, observing, and connecting. This is where you find the infamous oneness, one with the air that fills and leaves your lungs, and one with everything else. You may choose to spend some time in such a space. You are part of the Universe, and your space is part of all space.

In active meditation, we focus with *pure intention* on the outcome. We master *the practice* bit by bit. We make inner changes, and we create, visualize, and program ourselves to bring about change in our lives. We perform small miracles from within. From a young age, many of us are told we can do whatever we put our minds to. First, we believe, and then we develop the determination. We have the desire, persistence, and will. We magnetize it from within ourselves. The key is to ensure it is coming from a pure heart, aligned with higher self, and serving the greater good. If not, if there is any harm done or excessive attachment, giving your power and happiness to something outside of yourself, then there will be inner turmoil and suffering, often referred to as bad karma. The good news about this inner turmoil, however, is the value found that leads back to the roads of your higher intentions and dreams.

Upon taking a deeper look within, you may realize some buried subconscious intentions that have always been there. This is a close relative of intuition, the imprints and blueprints of your soul. You may get the sense of everything guiding you toward your highest intention and soul purpose. You may get the sense it has been happening all along. This is a matter of awakening. What if you are never not living your dreams? What if you are always living your dreams? What if you are living your dreams right now? What if everything you have been through has been part of living and realizing your dreams? What would you do differently?

To set your intention for spiritual growth in your workouts, start by taking a look at yourself, your life, and how you feel about yourself and your life. Your intention will depend on where you are. What do you bring with you for the day's workout? What feelings, weight, stresses, or worries do you carry? What are you facing in your life – what lessons are waiting to be acknowledged? What decisions need to be made? Are there any relationships that need some love? Ask yourself how you feel when you wake up, drive to the gym, or prepare for your workouts. While we all have our tendencies, this can vary day to day as different states of being. Whatever you bring with you is a starting point for an intention-based workout. From there, you develop your workout intention for the day. Ask yourself where you would like to be and how you would like to feel by the end of your workout. What is missing within you? What do you want to have more of in your life? Vulnerability is found in setting your intention, naming what your heart wants. The options are endless. What will you ask for and allow into your life?

Regardless of what state you find yourself in, there is one direction you are headed: up, lifting and releasing, becoming

Joy
laughter
fun
peace

stronger and lighter in spirit through your practice. Whether you feel down or on top of the world, all the more reason to continue. No matter what is happening in your life, whether perceived as good or bad, it can bring you closer to your highest good. May you find that for yourself whenever needed or wanted.

Whatever your intention, your practice is an opportunity and method to get there. If you seek clarity about something in your life, set the intention for *the workout* to help uncover it. Trust that you have the answers deeper within, that by the end of your workout, by the time you sit down and close your eyes, you will have clarity. If you are tired, set the intention for *the workout* to help wake you up. If you are dealing with an ailment, set the intention for *the workout* to be rehabilitative. Set the intention that you are cleansing as you sweat and rehydrate, that everything you are doing is helping you reach your goals, that you are letting go of excess weight, or that you are gaining muscle and bone density. Set the intention that you are healthy. If you are feeling down or lacking energy, set the intention for an emotional release, to raise your vibration, and gain energy as you exert yourself. Most simply, you can set the intention to be in a better place by the end of *the workout.*

As a form of positive thought and intention, mantras and affirmations can be repeated in meditation and your workouts to aid in concentration and help support your higher intentions. Affirmations are best stated in the present versus stating something for the future. They are also best phrased as a positive verses a negative statement. Imagine pushing yourself physically while quietly or silently repeating, "I am creating a life I love." Whatever it may be for you – becoming a better mother or father, wife or husband, or simply a happier, truer version of yourself – it is happening with your intention.

Processes for Reference

3

Presence

❖

"RIGHT HERE, COME on, Rich! Wake up in there!" I appeal to my friend, reaching in to touch his heart and soul, appealing to his higher self to transform any suffering into strength and greater presence. It's an inside job, and I am in process-delivery mode. Suffering paints his face from the shock of sensations and perhaps the dread of the remaining workout. He is resisting what is taking place.

"Smooth it out. Deep breaths. Breathe. This requires all of you. What are you made of? How do you want to do this?" I present *the call*.

The grimace of pain and resistance shifts to a grimace of surrender and determination. His eyes change. The fire is lit. He leans in and embraces *the challenge*. No matter how long it takes and no matter what physical and mental sensations are flooding his system, he finds a greater presence within himself, and he presses on.

In my own experiences, presence is when I place my hands on the bar and shift my eyes from glazed over, gazing in the distance, into sharp focus on the barbell in front of me, breathing energy into my body, and summoning all of myself to attempt a heavy squat.

Presence is eyeing a stack of plates on a wooden box that stands almost as tall as me. Without heightened presence, a jump like this would not be safe. Committed to the moment, I take two deep breaths followed by one big step to plant my feet while reaching back to gather explosive strength and momentum. I swing my arms into the air and launch myself as high as possible, pulling my legs up tightly to my chest. My toes land lightly on the edge of the stacked plates as I roll forward and stand up.

Presence is planting my hands firmly on the ground and kicking my legs up until they are straight over my head, my body firm while I relax into presence and balance. "Relax," I say to myself. No need to panic, simply to sense any subtle moves and walk, placing one hand in front of the other.

Presence is feeling the speed rope spinning rapidly twice around my body with each jump as I slow within myself to find the rhythm. Jump, swoosh, swoosh; jump, swoosh, swoosh; jump, swoosh, swoosh.

Presence is saying "No!" to feeling spent halfway through an intense workout, the arrival of a higher presence and a stronger version of myself.

Meditative fitness is presence, engaging all that is within you, and giving it to the present moment. The journey, the experience of the moment, is the essence of *meditative fitness. The practice* begins with intention and presence, each moment an opportunity in time. Presence is taking an eraser to the past and future that plays out in your heart and mind. Presence is simply being, and it is also being true to yourself: real and genuine, facing truth, embracing your heart and all that you feel. The layers of presence in these pages, encompassing *the four key areas of being*, include mindful presence (being present in the moment), heart and soul level presence (inherent within us all), and the greater presence elicited by meditation and fitness (finding something more within yourself).

Meditation asks for your presence, and *the workout* asks for your presence. Being present allows you to fully experience your life and seize transcendent opportunities. This leads to wisdom and understanding on the spiritual path. With presence also comes heightened awareness and memory. The more present you are, the more you will remember things in your life. Presence is found in the concentrated focus of intention, and greater presence is found in *pure intention*.

Presence during *the workout* is instrumental for maximum strength and higher performance. Prior to executing a big *lift*, weightlifters bring themselves into a presence of strength. Days when we are lacking this greater presence within ourselves are days when we slack or shy away from physical exertion, as though we don't want to confront the sensations. As a result, we don't feel as good at the end of *the workout*. When you finish a set, or whenever you have a chance in *the workout*, with your eyes open or briefly closed, breathe and incorporate greater presence, stepping into your strength. With this level of presence in your workouts, focus your thoughts, energy, breathing, and heart. You are there for every moment, mindful of the engagement.

The greater the physical challenge, the greater presence is evoked. When you witness someone working hard in a humble, endearing way, you see this greater presence. The purpose and power of being in their movement inspires others. None of this means we have to push ourselves to the point of injury or past physical safety, but we are still able to be fully present with commitment to the moments of our training. We may not lift our heaviest weight or go all out all of the time, but we can still devote all of ourselves. Whether it's strength training or metabolic conditioning, you can give your full attention. Even when your heart rate isn't maxed out, you can still dedicate all of your presence and be completely present with what you are doing. And when there is rest, there is meditative opportunity to transition and transfer to the physical exertion.

Whenever you find yourself waiting is the perfect time to meditate, sitting or standing wherever you are with your eyes open or closed for a moment. Meditation eliminates waiting and boredom. Gather your energy within yourself with a deep breath and slowly let it fall. When you raise your awareness to what is going on within you (your energy, thoughts, and deeper feelings), you realize there is a lot going on inside, and it is far from boring. Your spiritual life is breathtaking.

How present are you in your life? How asleep or awake, conscious or unconscious? Here or distant? Confronting or escaping? What might you be running from? What will you turn and face? What truths lead to your freedom and greater presence?

We can either be spaced-out and gone or tuned in, focused, and fully here. Many of us can admit to seeking escape in some form or another. Denial of suffering works on a particular level and is common, yet it can be equally as painful, for in order to be truly free of suffering, we must acknowledge it and move through to where true strength and joy live.

Presence helps us go from where we are to where we want to be. Presence is forward motion, letting go of the familiar and our comfort zones. If there is a lack of presence in your life, you are likely to find yourself stuck. Does every day seem the same? Do you wonder why the same things keep happening in your life? Presence is facing yourself, throwing away avoidance, escape, and denial. It is being able to stand in an inner strength no matter what is happening, even when you are brought to your knees. Strength is found in surrender, vulnerability, and the type of presence in these pages – the presence that will take your performance toward joy and brilliance.

If we want to conquer something, we don't avoid that something. Consider the sensations in a high-intensity workout that we would like to overcome. If we try to avoid these, our performance suffers. We can try to divert our minds and think about something else, or we can be fully present and embrace them so they don't control us anymore. We lean into them and make peace with them as another sensation, another beautiful experience we get to feel as human beings. We can either shrink in the face of physical discomfort or expand and transcend *the body*. We can be large in spirit through the physical exertion, rising to *the challenge*.

You can practice developing presence in any waking moment. How would you like to be able to walk into a room and, without saying a word, fill the entire room with energy and life? This is not to be confused with being an introvert or extrovert. Presence is noticeable as an inner light and radiance, and all of us can embody as beautiful a presence as any other living thing. Without doing or saying anything outwardly, we are able to fill a space through our presence, and we may lift the spirits of others simply by being there. If our presence alone makes a difference, think how much more is possible. The choice is ours. We either destroy faith in humanity or restore faith in humanity; we give energy or we drain energy; we offer life to others or we take it away any time we act as though ours is more important than theirs. We can choose to fill a space with peace, love, joy, and true strength, bringing out the best in others with our presence.

How would you like to fill your space?

Start from where you are and go from there.

How large or small do you feel on the inside?

How bright is your inner light burning?

What presence do you embody?

What do you radiate to the world?

No matter what, you have the ability to influence and change your state of being – mentally, emotionally, physically, and spiritually. We are humbly responsible for our state of being.

A lack of presence means we miss out on our precious lives. A lack of presence might mean that we are stuck in our heads rather than opening our hearts, and a lack of presence can be dangerous in *the workout* environment. Absent-mindedness is found at the root of accidents and injuries. Not paying attention to our form compromises our safety. If your back is crooked or rounded, then your spine is in jeopardy during a *lift*. If we don't pay attention in the midst of heavy weights, we may find out how much damage they can do. All it takes is a momentary lapse to put yourself in harm's way, to walk under a falling barbell or drop a weight on your foot.

As you practice meditation and fitness, it is important to be present with what you are doing. There are times to allow your mind to wander or to purposely explore your imagination. Great creativity can be found at such times. But even during these times, you can still be present within the wandering. The idea is for meditative practices to help us be more alert and focused; however, it is possible for inner work to take you out of presence, getting lost within yourself. For example, let's say you are taking a post-workout meditative shower,* relaxing your nervous system, aiding your recovery from a strenuous workout, allowing the water to cleanse you inside and out, washing away stress and any cloudy energy. And the next thing you know, you let your mind wander and can't recall whether you washed your hair. You got lost in the meditation, and you lost the connection with what you were doing. Instead, it is possible to incorporate any activity with intention and presence. Washing your hair becomes part of the cleansing meditation, and you are present for every aspect of the meaning-assigned act.

While this is a harmless example, it only takes one lost moment for something harmful to happen. Fortunately, *the workout* has a way of bringing us into the present moment. We often have no choice but to focus our efforts when exerting ourselves physically, and when safety is of the essence, we tend to snap into presence. As a general rule, whenever you catch yourself distant or distracted, bring yourself back to the moment. If you ever catch yourself zoning out, with your eyes losing focus, these are triggers to bring yourself back into focus. This is one of the most simple practices – bringing yourself back into presence, back to your breath, back to where you are and what you are doing. From this presence, you can visit the past and envision the future. You can go wherever you like and bring yourself back again. You are most powerful when fully present.

Presence holds the keys to your relationship with time. It changes how you experience time. Do you ever find yourself racing the clock through your day or workout as if you don't have enough time? Ever feel like the faster you go, the faster time goes? Your mind is racing as though time is running out – better hurry, hurry, go, go, go, come on, come on, no time, not enough time, running around in a constant state of inner panic. Rushing and hurrying is often one step away from irritability and anger when things don't go your way. You end up forcing your way through life, which is a weaker state of resistance. These moments provide opportunities to awaken to the stresses you place on yourself. Grounding to the present moment is how you take advantage of the opportunity. Slow time by slowing yourself. Relax and go to that inner space where you have as much time as you need to do what needs to be done. Whenever needed, let go of time as a constraint on happiness – time of day, time of year, time of life.

May we all slow down as often as possible, pause with our breath for a moment, and relax within ourselves whenever we need to. Even in a high-intensity workout, you can slow down inside. You can calm yourself as you push yourself. You can find peace in the exertion, being present in the moment instead of counting down to the end. This is about fluid movement through life and *the workout,* enjoying all the breaths along the way.

Grounding is the act of bringing yourself into presence. In meditation, you can practice grounding within your body, grounding on Earth, grounding to your breath, and more. As part of your practice, various types of grounding breaths can be used throughout your days and workouts. Gather energy within yourself. One breath can be enough, breathing from all around you, then down from the top of your head to the ground below. You can use your hands by bringing them up, level with the top of your head, palms facing down, and then lowering them with your exhale until your arms are extended with your hands parallel to the ground. While standing straight, send energy through your hands and feet before bringing your hands back up with your palms facing up and toward you as you breathe in and flow back within yourself. In this way, you can also gather strength for *lifts* and *movements.*

In life, one can be rooted in many things such as faith, religion, God, spiritual practice, work, family, sports, health, or fitness. If I am grounded in Christ, then Christ is present with me, and I am present with Christ. An ungrounded individual is difficult to connect with and may be described as having his or her head in the clouds, living in a fantasy or in denial, absent-minded, or disconnected. The grounded individual is often described as connected, down to earth, humble, based in reality, and present. The grounded individual, being present to others, is easier to communicate with, and better communication equals higher affinity and understanding.

The workout serves as an exercise in grounding, helping to create a foundation in your life. When engaging in a fitness regimen, are we not more likely to be making other healthy decisions? The odds are with us. The first day back after a long break is an act of re-grounding in health and fitness. Each workout serves as a positive choice to do something good for ourselves – an act of love.

When we are attached or addicted, clinging and holding on tightly, we are rooted in the addiction, which ultimately equals suffering. Different from healthy grounding, attachment or addiction to *the workout* hurts your *meditative fitness* practice. Instead, all you have is a problem, the inner turmoil of missing a workout or "having" to get in your workout to maintain sanity, holding on so tightly to control that everything has to be just right, which it never seems to be, in order for you to be happy. Many of us have been experienced masters of this recipe for unhappiness.

To be true to the essence of a *meditative fitness* practice, you mustn't be dependent on *the workout* for your happiness. Above all, *the practice* is your way of life, and you know you will continue in your way of life. No jeopardy. No fear of losing. Only being happy right now, no matter the circumstances. If something causes you to miss a workout, choose to be at peace rather than in turmoil. Choose to be grateful rather than resentful, because you know it is not something you have to do, but something you get to do, and you know you will make it for your next workout very soon. Allow the missed workout to fuel your motivation rather than bring you down. Ebbs and flows in your training and spiritual practice are to be expected. Trust that something greater is always in the works. The flow of life dictates when it is aligned for *the workout*, when it is within your control, and when it is not. None of this is an excuse to rationalize and overly abandon your practice. It is about finding freedom, balance, and alignment. When centered and grounded in your practice, you can enjoy resting your body as much as moving it in *the workout*. Everything is okay. Everything is okay right now. Nothing else needs to be done other than being happy right now.

The workout gives us the opportunity to empty ourselves, giving all of our heart and presence so we can receive renewed heart and spirit. In spiritual practice, with a beginner's mind, we empty ourselves to be filled by the presence of now. If we are so full of everything we know or constantly seeking to be right, we miss what the present moment has for us.

Passion can be found with ease in a presence-filled workout. The process is simple. To watch yourself train powerfully with purpose and presence, as you go through your workout, silently repeat to yourself:

"Who am I?"

"What am I made of?"

Allow *the workout* to become the prayer. Allow all else to drop away – no past, no future, only your presence, the physical exertion, and what it represents to you in the moment. As you repeat this, appeal to your highest self to wake up. Appeal to your faith, and open your heart. Ask for whatever you want in those moments when you are pushing yourself. Love. Peace. Joy.

Gratitude. Forgiveness. Strength. Compassion. Ask as though they are freely yours. Asking, allowing, and thanking all at once.

What do you believe you deserve?

And what do you believe is in store for you?

To be happy? To be fulfilled?

Or to suffer? Unfulfilled.

For some, your answers may surprise you when you are brutally honest with yourself, but if you can acknowledge and feel your truth, you can raise your frequency and vibration. If you have resigned yourself to believe that you will never have a truly fulfilling life, if you believe you deserve to suffer, such as when "bad" things happen and you tell yourself you deserve it, go ahead and suffer for as long as you like. You might as well get it over with. Punish yourself and suffer to your heart's content, and then, when you are ready, choose something better. Give yourself permission to, first, feel pain, and then to feel joy. The end of suffering waits for you. The presence of love and peace waits for you.

Greater presence, closely linked with your heart, helps you to see, listen, and feel more clearly. You may speak with heart and presence or without, filling the air with truth or with noise. The most important step toward truth is simply being true to yourself. You are the one who knows, the one who can connect with the part of you that is real on the inside.

In these moments of presence, you know exactly what to do and where to go, whether in meditation or your workouts. You sit down to meditate, and with presence, you flow from one aspect of the meditation to another. Without thinking about where you are going, you are already there. As you gain experience, not all workouts need to be precisely planned provided you have the starting vision. You can start with one or two core *lifts* or *movements* and go with *the workout* to see where it takes you. You can flow from *movement* to *movement*, increasing intensity as you go, creating strength and conditioning. Listen with presence, go with what comes to you, and find yourself in the flow of a meditative workout.

The art of listening stems from presence, wisdom, and humility. There are many forms of listening, whether to oneself (mind, body, heart, and soul), others (family, coach, teacher, or peer) or the Divine. As you flow from *movement* to *movement,* listen to your body, energy, and lungs to know how hard to push as you increase intensity. Listen to the world around you. Listen to the feedback and intuition in your movement to know where to make adjustments. Listen to your thoughts and your heart. Listen to the Universe.

Deep listening for higher inner guidance requires trusting yourself, your heart, and intuition, trusting what you know to be true. You can trust your inner wisdom. You can have faith in yourself as you connect with something greater within. Simply and only listen. Determine the source. Is it you and your ego, your past, or the expectations of others? Or is it something greater, like whispers from God or the Universe? Act on, rather than ignore, the guidance and intuition. Observe the results, and continue to gain wisdom and confidence.

How do you know when you are fully present? Your eyes are in focus and you can sense it throughout. You are at peace residing in your own skin, doing exactly what you are doing, like right now. You are reading or listening and your attention is on the words...right...now. There is no avoidance and your mind is not elsewhere. The past and the future are happening right now. You are right here, right where you are. You are home within yourself, with an open heart, and the lights are on.

Processes for Reference

Awareness

MY EYES OPEN. I'm awake. Gently rising out of bed, I turn to pull the quilt over the pillows. As soon as Allie hears this, she jumps up and buries her head in the covers while wagging her tail in the air, preventing me from properly making the bed. I welcome her morning ritual by ruffling her red hair and giving her some love. Only then am I permitted to cover the pillows before continuing my morning ritual. I grab my sandalwood beads and a small wooden mallet from the nightstand. I place the beads around my neck and gently tap the mallet on the side of a singing bowl – the signal of the meditation that is today. Tonight before bed, I will repeat these steps in reverse order.

Allie and her herding sister, Stella, fall back to sleep, awaiting their morning trek. On my feet now, my legs feel strong, and I feel light as a result. The soreness from my previous days' practice provides evidence of hard work, a satisfying feeling. I give these areas an extra stretch as I spread my arms like wings and reach up to the sky. Blood flow sparks from my chest to my fingertips, all the way to my toes, tingling throughout my body. Individual cells are awakening too.

I'm grateful for the noticeable difference between days like these and days when I have woken up groggy, heavy, and tired. From the moment I wake up, my practice begins. The way you feel when you wake up can be spiritually revealing, a starting point for your daily practice. With awareness, I start from where I am. Whether waking up light or heavy, happy or sad, peaceful or anxious, there is an ongoing choice to be made.

I pause, tune in, and connect with my breath. I breathe in, ground, and expand my awareness to the world around me, creating a foundation for my state of being. Energy flows, seemingly automatic, breath by breath, up and down my spine. From here, I know I can do many things. Today, like every day, has meaning and opportunity.

As I make my way to the kitchen, I again notice a lightness afoot. Ah, to be moving. My heart knows I feel this good because I have been taking care of myself. I relish days like this, when my energy is clear. I am happy, something that once felt so elusive. I am happy to have the courage to be me and to continue to awaken daily. It feels like choosing to be alive.

Proceeding to the fridge for some water, I look forward to the first glass of the day. Water serves every cell, aiding blood flow, energy, and more. With the first gulp, the unique sensation of cold water descends on my empty stomach, filling me up inside, and rushing to help everything work more fluidly.

"What would do me good this morning?" I ask.

"Awake energy," I whisper with my hands around the glass, "and love for myself and others."

With a meditative intention-prayer, I add this to the water and take another awakening gulp. Love and energy flood my body. I employ this water-intention practice* before, during, and after workouts and meditations, as well as throughout the rest of the day. It has gotten to the point where subconscious blessings are always with the water. As in the previous examples of clearing energy and releasing knots, knowing I needed all the help I could get for those small miracles, I applied this practice. Not only does hydration help physically, it can help metaphysically as well. What a funny little practice, water as a conductor of energy and intention, where science meets spirituality.

Within a few minutes, Allie, Stella, and I are out for our meditative morning walk around the lake, where I practice being happy and radiating bliss to others as they cross my path.

"This is what I desire to take with me out in the world," I say to myself.

As I walk, I can focus my attention and awareness on the ground under my feet or the sound of the electric train in the distance. I can focus on the ducks playing chase or other walkers passing by. I can focus on the shadows in my mind, the shadows created by the sun, or the reflections floating on the water. I can focus on the wind that reminds me of God, a presence I cannot see, but feel. I can focus on a spot in the distance and expand my awareness to my peripheral vision. I can expand around and behind me while still looking at the spot. Right now, I focus on awareness itself; I am aware that I am aware.

Is there anything not encompassed by awareness? Where does awareness begin? Does it have a beginning or an end? Awareness of awareness of awareness. Infinite awareness. And there we are.

Reflecting upon my first two fitness adventures at Tiger's Den, I remember being aware of the inner process of thoughts, feelings, and sensations. *The workout* heightens intention, presence, and awareness. When my oxygen-starved body screamed at me and my breaths became hyperventilating gasps – shallow, tight, chaotic, and desperate – awareness led me to doing something about it. I was responsible for my breathing. I was the one creating that less-than-ideal oxygen delivery. As soon as this consciousness arose, I went into a *meditative state* to deepen my breathing and calm myself so I could continue.

As I executed the *lifts* and as I ran, I was aware of my body positions and running posture. I glanced to my right as I passed some industrial shops. A couple of men hauled equipment from their truck across the street, apparently arriving from some off-site industrial job. It's funny how our minds work: I have no idea what they were doing, but based on my perception, that was the instant story I told myself. At the same time, I heard the sound of my feet hitting the pavement and the rhythm of my breath. The wind created by the run felt cool against my skin. I found myself deep in thought, less conscious of the outside world. Upon that realization, I brought myself back into presence and back to the run. Awareness showed me the way.

Meditative fitness is awareness, expanding and awakening from within. *The practice* begins with intention, presence, and awareness – the third segment of this powerful triangle. Each side supports the other to help transform *the workout* (or any other chosen activity) into a spiritual engagement. In exercising these elements, you raise your spiritual intelligence. Awareness is with us when we set intention or connect with presence. When our mind wanders, when we lose presence, awareness guides us back. It is the essence of our being and nature of our souls, ever expanding like the Universe, and always with us.

The infinite layers and types of awareness range from physical senses to metaphysical senses, from the physical body to energy, thoughts, feelings, beliefs, intuitions, truth, and karma. We have inner and outer senses, and we can also have selective senses, either paying attention to sights and sounds or not paying attention. A *meditative state* heightens our senses, and spiritual practice helps develop our sensitivity. Through the inherent awareness found in presence, you may observe all that takes place inside and out. Practice turning your senses inward while still perceiving everything around you. Train yourself to be narrowly focused while widely aware – *pure intention* with expanding awareness. You are aware of your inner world as well as every movement, sight, sound, touch, taste, and smell. Incorporate and invite all as part of the meditation, at peace and one with your surroundings.

The present moment is recorded in your soul. Your subconscious receives more stimuli than you can consciously process in each passing moment. We are aware in ways we don't always realize, either conscious (awake) or unconscious (asleep) to this eternal awareness. When we allow deeper awareness to heighten our consciousness and our perceptions, we enter a world of possibilities.

Awareness rises from within as though everything is simply waiting to be realized.

Intuition is a form of inner awareness, but it is a sense we don't always choose to trust. Some intuitions take time to develop and recognize as more than a temporal notion. One question to ask is: "What have I always known about myself?" On the side of good – with God and all that is good – what you have always known about yourself is true. And if you have doubted or denied yourself, there is no need to doubt or deny anymore.

Awareness shines light in darkness. When you come to know something, there is no turning back. More than memory, once you are spiritually aware, you are forever changed, and you can never again not know. Awareness calls us to action. Once the light of awareness arrives, if you continue to go against your true nature and what you have come to know, it can feel like selling your soul. When we are aware of hurting ourselves or someone else and continue to do so, we dig a deeper and darker hole than if we were unaware. From here, the light of awareness still shines the way out.

Spiritual awakening is a process of rising awareness. In spiritual practice, we become aware of what is happening under the surface. We experience lightbulb and aha moments, wins, inner victories, and self-realization. We continue to integrate our soul perfection. We raise our consciousness and in turn raise our vibration, the frequency on which we operate. It is up to each of us to cultivate our awareness, and there are infinite layers and infinite ways to awaken.

What do we wake up from? From hurting ourselves and others; from suffering; from being dead inside; from spiritual blindness, denial, or ignorance of the truth; from being sick, tired, lethargic, and heavy. We wake up from depression, addiction, and attachment; from unhappiness and unfulfilled lives.

We wake up to being alive with heart and healthy passion. We wake up to the end of suffering; to living in light; to truth, intuition, soul purpose and perfection; to our actions and karma. We wake up to a higher power and our true higher selves: love, peace, joy, kindness, compassion, Christ-consciousness, or our inherent Buddha nature.

Awareness can change everything. It can help you develop flexibility of behavior to get better results in any area of life. Recognizing when something isn't working, you are provided the opportunity to do something different. Spiritual practice and personal growth increase our levels of self-awareness. Some problems or inner conflicts simply disappear once they are brought to light. Expanding awareness alone equals growth. At the same time, awareness by itself doesn't change your circumstances. It does, however, change your perspective. It motivates you to make the change, and it gives you the power to modify behaviors, set intentions, and take action. Awareness accompanied by positive intention and action equals wave after wave of growth.

Awareness of your karma is helpful on your path. Perhaps the simplest definition of karma is ongoing cause and effect. This doesn't have to be a mystical concept, however there are many different kinds of karma. In essence, everything, including the entire workings of the Universe, have led to right now. All the compounding decisions you have made (actions and inactions), and the way you have responded to all that has happened in your life, has led to where you are now. We create our lives. If you eat as much as you can all day, there is a good chance you will gain weight. If you don't get out of bed for three days, there is a good chance you will be depressed. If you regularly seek lightbulb moments, you will end up with a whole lot of light. If you constantly envision yourself a certain way, good or bad, you're likely to bring it to fruition.

The following questions help reveal your karma and perhaps some karmic cleaning that could be done, but first, please know: the fact you are reading this means you already have good karma. The journey has long been underway.

Do you like where you are in your life? Do you like who you are? Do you love your life? Do you create friends or enemies? Are you calm and centered or reactive? Does life press your buttons? What is happening inside of you? What is happening in your life? Do you keep yourself in stress and worry? Do you live in fear and avoidance, constantly running from things? Are there people, circumstances, or life events that haunt you, hold you back, or weigh you down? What drives you? What were the defining moments of your life when everything changed and life began a new course? And how have you responded?

This is your journey, and this karmic awareness will help guide you on your path, providing spiritual work for your practice. It requires humble honesty, acknowledging truths you may not want to admit.

What are you willing to admit to yourself?

How often do you lie to or fool yourself?

What do you believe about yourself?

And how do you know it's real and true?

One way to know is by doing the deep, inner, heart-level work. Truth resonates in your soul. In your spiritual life, you learn how to know whether something is true for you. We all have access to this innate awareness to help guide us through our practice. On one hand, we have our current beliefs about ourselves. On the other hand, we have more self-realization waiting to happen. In between the two is your path toward a more enlightened life.

You can either behave in a way that supports your workouts and practice or behave in a way that does not. You can either be causal or be at effect. You can either take ownership and responsibility, or be a victim and give away your power. Here is the great news – what you do now determines where you will be in the future. You can transform and master your karma starting right now. One meditation alone can transform your karma. You will begin to see that certain realities are only possible if you do this or do that, applying to both the good and the bad. You see the path, and the path is continually revealed.

The more you grow in your meditative awareness, the more you will know what to do in your workouts, how hard to push, how to manage your energy, when to slow down or increase intensity, and how to best use your breath. In *meditative fitness,* awareness unlocks potential and helps you develop your intuitive athleticism. Be wary of limiting beliefs. Whenever we say we can't do something, we limit ourselves. In the heart of physical exertion, awareness tells us we are capable of more. It tells us we are stronger than we think we are, and it also helps keep us safe.

In your practice and in completing the processes following these chapters, you will develop numerous personal techniques to enhance your awareness. This has already begun. To continue, pause, look within, and sense with all of your being.

You have the ability to tune in and recognize your state of being at all times. You know the state you embody when you enter a workout. With ongoing and daily awareness, you set your intention. Practice the habit of checking in with yourself. From there, set sights on something greater than your smaller self and rise to a higher state. Awareness lets you know whether your heart and mind are aligned with strength and clarity.

A meditative workout is overflowing with awareness, and you choose what to do with it. When a muscle tightens, you either contribute to the tightness or do something to change it. Rather than focusing on the tension, focus on relaxing or shaking it out. Rather than focusing on how fast your heart is beating, focus on slowing it down. Rather than focusing on not being able to breathe, focus on delivering oxygen efficiently. Be aware, pay attention, and focus accordingly. We attract that which we focus, and that which we focus perpetuates. You are aware when you hit a wall in *the workout*, and you can concentrate on how you can't continue, or you can concentrate on doing what you need to do to keep going. Practice steady awareness to continue to reach new heights.

Envision being aware of your performance and any room for improvement. You know when a *movement* feels right, when *lifts* are executed well, and when they are not. You are aware of your relative strength for the day and whether your movement is clumsy or coordinated. You are aware of your balance, especially when you start to lose it. You realize weaknesses to transform into strengths. You are aware when your muscles are near failure, aware of how to break up sets and plan or pace *the workout*, when to rest, when you are leaving too much in the tank, and when you are going through the motions rather than engaging passionately. You are aware of the barbell, the weight in your hands, how to move the weight, when your form is strong, and when it is lazy. You are aware of all of your mental choices. You are conscious of your mobility or lack thereof, and keeping yourself safe. You are aware of your true physical limitations rather than falsely conceived ones, which is an expanding awareness. You know how high or how far you can jump. You are aware of your breathing, heart rate, and other physical sensations, the clock, the crowd, and fellow athletes. You are aware of the burning sensation in your lungs and muscles. You are aware of sweat dripping from your body, your wet clothes, the music in your ears and the music in your soul, the grunts and noises made by yourself and others, and the sounds of weights dropping. You are aware of the foods you have been putting into your body, feeling the results in your workouts. You are aware of your thoughts, emotions, and energy, and when you are balanced, centered, and aligned.

There are no limitations or restrictions on your practice. You can have a meditative moment in your workout whenever it enters your awareness.

If you question your level of awareness, all you need to do is pay attention, and you will start to notice. Pay attention and become aware whenever you are carrying undue tension, and develop the habit of releasing inner pressure. At any point in *the workout* and especially in the stillness of a post-workout meditation, you may feel something beautiful wash over you like a wave of energy and endorphins, contributing to a sense of well-being. More than that, you will receive whatever you are willing to allow, whatever matches your vibration in those precious moments.

Processes for Reference

5

Thought

"This should be fun!" The thought bursts out of me to those within earshot as I study the team workout of the day. Also written on the board is the word "EGO" with a big X through it. No room for ego here. *The workout* knows how to take care of an inflated ego. The environment at Tiger's Den is one of community and shared vulnerable experiences, a contrast from my local gym. We are in this journey together. Athletes introduce themselves to newcomers with handshakes and a sense of unity. Hugs, high fives, and fist bumps are common. All those here have taken a significant step for the day, especially those here for the first time. The simple act of showing up is courageous. Each workout, vigorously moving your body and lifting heavy objects, requires commitment and courage.

"What's this last part?" I bug Collin.

"I'll show you. All athletes over here, huddle up!" he calls out. When the teams are assigned, I am paired with two gentlemen of similar fitness levels, who, not surprisingly, are quite a bit larger in size than me.

Collin goes over the squats, sit-ups, and lunges, demonstrating the standard of movement for each one. I am confident with bodyweight *movements*, so I think this should be a fairly easy workout. When he gets to the last part, however, he leans over, grabs the wrist and leg of another athlete, and hoists that athlete onto his shoulders. My heart skips a beat. It's happening too fast all of a sudden.

"Wait, wait, wait, we are to do what and how?" I question with wide eyes. I am to carry each teammate on my shoulders for multiple 100-meter "runs," and I'm no longer looking forward to this workout.

"How can I get out of this? I should just do my own training. I don't think I can carry those guys like that." Weak thoughts reel through my mind. I could easily let them get the best of me and talk myself out of it completely.

The three of us huddle toward the rear loading dock eagerly identifying our current weigh-ins. One is around 160 pounds, the other 170 pounds, and then there's me at 140 tops. Sometimes it pays to be small, and sometimes it does not. I could have them carry me the whole time, but that would defeat the purpose. Despite doubting my ability to do this, I am reminded of the many soldiers I have known and their testimonies of deployments, the many who touched my heart in sharing theirs. If I were carrying a battle buddy to safety when his life depended on it, if those were the stakes, would I have these shallow doubts? I think not.

My thoughts of doubt transform into thoughts of determination, which would not be what they are without being tested.

I must think strong. I am going to do this. I am going to carry these guys 100 meters on my shoulders, 25 meters at a time if I have to, and as many times as *the workout* demands.

The buzzer sounds, and the race is on. I begin squatting while my teammates take off with one on the shoulders of the other, creating quite the picture with the garage-size doors framing these wod warriors. Columns of human T's run away from the loading dock. Upon their return, my legs are burning from 57 squats. I jump down from the loading dock, and it's my turn to be carried. Sticking his shoulder in my abdomen and wrapping his arm around my leg, my teammate throws me up with ease as I am quickly airborne like a sack of potatoes. He powers across the spacious cargo lot. For me, the world is upside-down and sideways. I experience only a slight fear of being dropped and the discomfort of the bouncing shoulder lodged in my gut. All in all, however, I enjoy the ride, appreciating the rest and the sideways bouncing view of the world. To our left and to our right are other spectacles of athletes carrying each other, some with better success than others. Laughter is intermixed with grunts and groans and heavier than normal foot patter. Distances are spray-painted in black on the concrete. My chariot is strong, speeding along all the way to the 100-meter marker. When we get there, he nearly throws me aside in celebration as if I really was a sack of potatoes.

My turn. Step one: figure out how to get this nice, strong 160-pound fellow onto my shoulders.

"Here comes that level of commitment," I think to myself. "Commit to the *lift*, commit to the *lift*" goes the internal command.

I lodge my shoulder, grab his thigh, and hoist while he gives a little hop to assist. Somehow, he's up on my shoulders, curled around my neck, but something doesn't feel right, and he is certainly more than a sack of potatoes. He feels more like a grand piano, more than I imagined 160 pounds to feel like. My spine feels crooked like it could give at any moment, an indicator I must not be fully engaging my core strength. All of this adds up to two things: it is extremely challenging and the positioning is off.

"This is too hard. I'm not going to make it. Too heavy, not good for my spine; not gonna make it, better put him down," the rapid stream of weak thoughts get the best of me. I barely make it to the halfway point before I set him down. After 10 seconds or so, my brave and now intimate teammate is hoisted back onto my small frame. Finding the centered balance again proves difficult, but slowly, step-by-step, I arrive back to home base, temporarily spent. No time to waste though, our third is ready to switch and go, and we're off.

"Dang, you're light," he says, as he runs at a smooth pace. Before we know it, we arrive at his finish line – my dreaded starting line. We trade places. I grab his wrist and bend down to wrap my other arm around his thigh. A split-second later, I am overwhelmed with human weight on my shoulders – all 170 pounds of it. Each step is strained. Each breath is painful, and it's impossible to inhale deeply. I feel weak, lacking strength in conjunction with my impending weak thoughts. I make it 30 meters before pausing to readjust, feeling a sense of failure. We lose some valuable time after me struggling to hoist him back up, making it another 30 meters and stopping again, but still, I do it. I carry him and finish the 100 meters.

"How many more times do I have to do that?" I wonder. No way of knowing for sure as I am up to finish our team's sit-ups before moving on to lunges. This is the easy part. Whoever thought rest in *the workout* could be on the shoulders of another or in doing sit-ups? This redefines the term "*rest period*." I recover while completing 50 sit-ups and a dozen lunges until my teammates are back. We swap positions and I go for another 100-meter ride before turning around to play the role of the chariot. No more than walking heavily, I am constantly thinking of when to pause for rest and repositioning. I make it halfway, set my comrade down with care, stretch and straighten, and pick him back up. Onward. We make the rotation again, and the ride back over is full of processing thoughts as I'm bouncing up and down in the name of fitness and the benefit of all.

A new chain of thought arises from within while listening above. If I don't do something, I am going to end this workout with a sense of failure, and I won't feel good about my attitude and effort. As my turn rapidly approaches again, the thought appears – *stronger as I go*. I begin to repeat in my mind with ever-increasing will, "Think strong. I am getting stronger as I go, stronger as I go," and the mantra is born.

I get in position and hoist our heaviest teammate with good form. Immediately I notice it feels better. Still heavy, but the balance feels right, and my core is engaged. I start off slow, whispering with gentle strength, "Stronger as I go, stronger as I go, stronger as I go."

As I repeat these words in rhythm with my breath, I speed up to a heavy run, approaching the 50-meter mark, feeling strong with centered balance and no thoughts of stopping, only getting "stronger as I go." I am the mantra with *pure intention*. I continue to increase in speed and strength until I am sprinting through the finish line. *Pure intention* shifts to pure elation. I set my teammate down and celebrate like a running back who just scored the winning touchdown, with my arms flexed in front of me while stomping my feet. High fives and fist-bumps fly around.

"This is what it feels like to be strong," I think to myself. I am not sure I ever felt or saw myself that strong before, and I am in awe of going from a state of weakness to great strength, in an instant...with a single thought.

Meditative fitness is thought aligned with higher self. When our thoughts align with heart and intention, our bodies follow suit. With awareness, we are in tune with our thoughts. With intention, we focus our thoughts. With presence, our thoughts are grounded in the moment. Thoughts help create your experience, your beliefs, and your perceived reality. The experience is what matters rather than analyzing or figuring it all out. The journey happens in real time. Our thoughts determine whether we are caught in our perception of the past, present in the moment, or at an imaginary point in the future. We have thought our way to where we are in life, and we are always creating.

What are the stories you tell yourself? What dominates your thoughts? What will you create with your thoughts today? How will you direct your thoughts in your life and workouts?

We are powerful beings, and as a result, our thoughts are powerful as well. Positive thoughts turn *I can't do it* into *I am doing it,* and *I'm horrible* into *I am improving every second.* Thoughts can contribute to fears, doubts, and non-belief, or they can contribute to love, confidence, and faith. How easily we can get ourselves "worked up." We can think ourselves into worry, stress, and anxiety, or we can think ourselves into calm, peaceful relaxation. This is life, and it is always happening. In *the practice,* thoughts are a form of processing on the path to new realization. We train our thoughts and choose them wisely, for they play a determining role.

At the same time, a thought is just a thought. You are not your thoughts. Rather, you are something much greater. Rising thoughts need not have control. They come to be and they pass; they appear and they dissolve; new ones arrive in place of old; and patterns repeat. In meditation, we observe and re-pattern our thoughts. We assign the meaning and decide which ones matter. Our inner wisdom guides us to know the difference between just another thought and thoughts that change our lives.

Thoughts carry weight when the weight is given. It is your choice whether to align intention with a thought. Intention solidifies thoughts by giving them substance, and thoughts can also help support your intention. For example, I thought about going to the gym for a long time, but just recently had the intention of doing so. Or, my intention is to be healthy and happy, so I think about what I can do to support that.

With your thoughts, you can use your imagination and choose your mental energy. You can change and guide your direction. As in the above workout story, you can think your way weak or you can think your way strong. Your mind can wander and lose focus and presence, and your mind can come back and gain focus and presence. Whenever needed, re-center your thoughts during meditation and *the workout*.

Because our thoughts are powerful, they can also be a source of great suffering and mental illness. In my head is where insanity lives before my heart washes it away. Obsessive thinking can be brought on by unaddressed, underlying feelings, pressure rising to the surface. Many mental issues are emotional and spiritual puzzles to solve.

We attach ourselves to certain thoughts, buy into them, and give them weight, yet they are not always based in truth. We get stuck and latch on, replaying thoughts over and over, creating conflict, turmoil, and friction of the mind – the feeling of crazy. The energy is too much and can contribute to issues such as suicidal ideation, cutting, rage, eating disorders, addiction, anxiety, depression, and more. Our thoughts are not the only factor behind these issues, but they make a difference for better or worse. If you constantly think bad things are going to happen to you, then they will. You get what you look for, and even if nothing negative is happening, that is the way you might perceive it. Lower forms of thought carry a lower vibration, and this is how we attract and manifest our fears – that which matches the vibration of our thoughts and being. In your practice, you can learn how to liberate and direct your thoughts toward manifesting your dreams.

Thoughts create your beliefs and the stories you tell yourself. In many cases, you need to change the story to overcome limiting beliefs. These stories are often related to things you have lived with over time, such as your body, self-image, or troublesome physical ailments. As challenges for us to overcome in life, they can be connected to some of our greatest lessons. For years, I said, "I have bad knees" and "a chronic elbow problem." The first step toward changing and healing these joints was changing the story I was telling myself. I began to say things such as, "I have good knees. I have healthy elbows. I love you knees, I forgive you elbow. My knees and elbows are getting better all the time." I stopped believing in the old story, and the new story began to take shape. In combination with rehabilitative movement and mobility, pains miraculously disappeared, and my joints feel better now than ever before.

We have the ability to think ourselves into a better place. Let's say you are not doing well and you focus on the thought "I'm not doing well," perpetuating this direction. Upon deliberation, you decide to go for a meditative walk.* As you walk, you think about letting go, surrendering to the way you feel, flowing thoughts up to a higher power, and giving up the part of you that is not doing well, the thoughts, feelings, energy, and whatever is happening in your life. You imagine the struggle and conflict floating away. You think about how good you're going to feel, how good it feels to be doing what you are doing right now, and you are no longer thinking about...you can't remember what. You are only thinking about feeling good and that the energy is transforming, and that no matter what, the imbalance is balancing. Through those kinds of thoughts, your thoughts, you transform your experience.

This is more than positive self-talk, but that which is real and true to you. It has to be what works for you, something you can start with and believe in. So when you are having a hard time, examine your thoughts and patterns. Examine them to ensure they are not contributing to your misery. No one else has your answers, and this is about your thoughts, choosing them wisely, and choosing to transform to a better state with a higher vibration. Put your thoughts to work for you and something greater.

A common misconception about meditation is that your mind must go quiet. Often, beginning meditators meet this with resistance, trying to stop the thoughts or force their mind to quiet down. Even the word "must" implies force and carries the vibration. Only in allowing will we find a quiet mind. Similar to trying to remember something, when we stop forcing and trying to think of it, the memory appears. Although not a recommended primary practice, there is nothing wrong with letting your mind wander and seeing where it takes you. Before long, you may find yourself working out problems at a deeper, subconscious level.

It is important not to overthink, overanalyze, or judge your meditations, for this creates barriers to spiritual growth and can take you out of presence, out of your heart, and out of the flow of energy. Wisdom and true understanding are not found through intellectualizing, rather through direct experience. Nearly every meditator faces some unruly thoughts in their practice. You have two options when this is the case: You can continue until you feel a shift, or you may pause, reset, and re-enter the meditation. Either way, allow it all to serve as part of your training. You may encounter racing thoughts early in a meditation only to then have a life-changing experience with deep communion and bliss, tears of joy, and overwhelming peace. It won't be long before entering a *meditative state* becomes a matter of tuning in at will.

In your workouts, center your thoughts on the task at hand. Prior to *lifts* or *movements,* think about how you are going to execute. Think about your form and mentally rehearse the movement pattern. While executing, think about a specific cue such as "eyes up" or "drive through the heels." Think about how your body or the *movement* feels. Think about the end result, moving the weight to your shoulders or overhead. If you catch yourself complaining or getting frustrated, immediately flip that mental switch. Think positively. Bring yourself into strength with your thoughts. Think about how graceful and athletic your movement is. Think about summoning all of the strength within you to move the weight. Think about how strong you are simply for doing what you are doing. Think about how much good you are doing for yourself and others. Think about how you will inspire others with your effort.

In physical exertion, overthinking gets in the way of fluid movement. Thinking your way through a *movement* makes it clinical and forced rather than natural and athletic. Fluidity and coordination doesn't come from thinking your way through a motion. You can tell by an athlete's technique if they are over-thinking, like seeing the "swing thoughts" of a golfer in their swing. The motion becomes disconnected or exaggerated with a hitch. Prior to an intricate or technical *lift* or *movement,* think about the form, think about completing the *movement,* but when it comes time to do it, switch to feeling it. Feel the *movement* and execute with confidence. This is where it helps for coaches to use simple cues that connect with feeling. Take it a step further and find the one feeling that encompasses the most, a linchpin for everything coming together.

The less practiced we are, the more it seems like there is to think about. This is where drills come in, grooving movement patterns. Drill, drill, drill; process, process, process; program, program, program; and the next thing you know, you are able to do it without thinking. The same that applies in *the workout* applies in meditation as you recondition your mind and body. If you breathe up and down your body for 100 reps, moving your consciousness and energy, you will have programmed that ability.

Meditation and *the workout* can help break old patterns of thought and create new positive ones. We can't always control the negative thoughts that pop up, such as "I can't," or "I suck," or "these lunges suck," or "I hate burpees." Sometimes words like this pop out of our mouths before we even realize what we are saying, and a lot of times we don't really mean them, but somehow we feel better saying "I suck" when we are not happy with our performance. Perhaps because then, at least we let others know we're not happy with it, which therefore makes us more than what we just did, like "I won't settle for that. I will improve. I'm better than that." But then we really don't want to reinforce the story of "I suck." Instead, we would rather reinforce the humble story of, "I can do better," or "I am improving." When negative thoughts happen, without judgment or resistance, simply notice them, and redirect them toward the light.

We are very good at fooling ourselves with the help of our thoughts. The great thing about being able to fool yourself is that it works both ways – negative and blinding or positive and enlightening. If you tell yourself, "oh, this is going to be hard," or "this is going to be heavy," does that help you to complete the task? For your subconscious and nervous systems, you want to think easy and light. The best physical example of this is if you pick up a barbell at 250 pounds, then pick up a barbell at 135 pounds and notice how light it feels. This is the effect you want to create with the help of your meditative thoughts. Think your way to becoming stronger, lighter, and happier as you go.

After completing the formidable workout that had me carrying humans, I asked Scott for his impression on thoughts in *the workout.* He said, "Simple. Thoughts should be on the desired result! Think from the end! Think of others rather than yourself.

Be thoughtful rather than thoughtless. I like to think everything is unfolding perfectly rather than wanting things to be other than they are. Each *lift* and *movement* is perfect on the road of improvement and success. Rather than complain, I like to focus my thoughts on gratitude for being able to do all of it. I changed my life by changing my thoughts, and I like to inspire myself with my thoughts."

"What's the one thing you want others to know?" I asked.

"You have to experience it for yourself. And I'm excited for those who do," he said with a heartfelt smile.

Processes for Reference

6

Heart

As soon as I wake up, sinking into gravity, I feel it. I'm not happy. Something doesn't feel right. My heart is heavy. It's my birthday. I am 34 today, and there is an all-too-familiar absence of joy. Rare these days, but earlier in life, there were years spent with this absence; there was never a sense of well-being. From what I have come to learn, I know something significant is happening. My choice is to either stay in this unhappy space or to move through it. I know what I have to do. My heart will open and the river will flow.

"Thank you for allowing me to feel," I pray silently. Today is a day for *the workout,* and on this day, I will go to my local gym seeking a wide-open heart.

On my way, I reflect on the meaning of this day. Intuition tells me these are important years that will make a difference for the rest of my life, changing and expanding my karma. And despite recent positive energy, I still woke up unhappy. It doesn't always add up, and knowing how bad it can get, it still scares me when I feel this way. This fear, however, carries no real weight of its own, and what once was painful beyond bearing is now beautiful beyond measure. All I have to do is open my heart to all of it.

As I pass through the doors of my local facility, the young woman behind the counter looks up from the book she's reading.

"Good mmorrrrning!" she proclaims with a contagious smile.

"Morning, how are you today?" I smile back.

"Good, thanks." She takes my card.

"Whatcha reading there?" I ask, peeking over the counter.

"Oh, this? It's called *The Shack*."

"Oh, that's a special book. You'll have to let me know how you like it."

"I sure will," she says.

Regardless of what else is going on, I am genuinely happy to see her as a familiar, friendly face. Although I don't always live up to my own standards, I feel I owe it to others to be my higher self, to be kind and grant them their space in life, with permission to be themselves. When we cross paths, I offer the right of way. When encountering another soul, I can't help but observe and ask myself whether they are happy and fulfilled. Sadly and too often, the answer is no, not fully, not by the purest definitions. Many set the bar low, "happy" to make it through another day, or "happy" with temporary shallow pleasures and materialistic lives. When I was in a darker place, just hearing the word "happy" made me more depressed. Everything in life seemed to come easy except being happy. No matter how good things were, no matter what else was happening in my life, I couldn't see the point to any of it. "There has to be more than this," was the constant underlying feeling. I previously had no hope that happiness was possible for me, yet I was always sensitive in wanting it for others.

The practice is to observe without judgment. Of course in any moment, one may be more or less happy than others, but there is also a predominant, longer-term vibration. What is their energy saying? Are they having a moment or are they truly unhappy and unfulfilled? Either way, subconscious prayers and blessings accompany these observations, wishing there was more I could do, and there is. I first learned how to suffer deeply in order to learn how to live free of suffering. Before one helps others find happiness and fulfillment, one must first find these things for themselves, and so I continue my journey.

"Have a great workout today!" she says, handing me back my card.

"Thank you, I will," I respond, with my heart rising to my throat and welling in my eyes. "I'm ready to put my heart into it."

Walking down the center path that splits the facility in half, I expand my awareness and take in the entire floor. People move about from machine to machine. To my left are vacant rooms where various yoga, spinning, dance aerobics, and boot camp classes are conducted, which reminds me of a recent news report about a growing facility called "SoulCycle" that offers spiritual spin classes.

"The world is ready for more of that," the Universe whispers.

The early crowd has all but cleared, making the place a bit more conducive for *the practice*. The open space is filled with rows and rows of machines built for training various body parts. Floating above the ground, a woman climbs a revolving staircase.

From where she is, lifted above the main floor, the view consists of treadmills, free weights, machines, and other fitness contraptions. Throughout my life, I trained in innumerable facilities much like this one. They typically have everything one needs to create infinite combinations to move and work *the body*.

At the end of the middle path is a small nook, perfect for warming up, cooling down, and best of all, meditating. Black cushioned mats lie on the ground against mirrored walls. This space holds special meaning as though blessed and anointed. *The workout* will begin and end here.

I focus on my heart as I mobilize my body with dynamic stretches and a few yoga postures. There are pauses between stretches and while holding a posture. I take advantage of these little pauses, simply to breathe and feel, continuing to sink into the gravity of life and the weight on my heart. It is as though I can feel all of it all at once, the overwhelming entirety of life and the world at large. I know what is in my heart, waiting to come out and guide me to the light of my soul. Nothing feels better than surrender. Opening my heart has been such a powerful experience that it can be intimidating. There were days when all I felt was life-threatening pain and sadness, and I grew afraid to feel, not yet able to handle my heart. Everything I felt led me to wanting to take my life.

I was 12, but probably looked no more than eight or nine, just a little guy. I sat at the kitchen counter, struggling over some math homework, not wanting to do it in the first place. Already life was eating at me, and already I wasn't happy, feeling things beyond my years, sensitive and overwhelmed by it all. I distinctly remember turning around and saying to my mom, "I wish I was dead," with all the intention in my being. That wish stayed with me as a constant companion for the next 17 years. When I hit 16, the wish peaked and I began to obsess over how I was going to kill myself. After two years of thinking about it every day, never speaking it to another soul, I thought I had found my answer. I drove home from school and parked a large 1975 Checker Marathon in the garage and left it running. I had already written a short note dividing up my small number of prized possessions, letting everyone know I loved them and that I would be in a better place. That day was the day I was going to kill myself. It took me two years to build up to it, and I only lasted around 15 minutes before I turned the car off. Two years obsessing about it every day, and I couldn't do it. Not only did I not want my mom to be the one to find me, but something else stopped me, something I didn't yet recognize. Immediately following, I felt even more lost. I went inside and stood in front of the bathroom mirror for the next 45 minutes, talking to myself between waves of tears.

"What are you going to do now? That was your only plan. If you can't kill yourself, and you know you can't keep living this way, with the way you feel...then, you have to change. You have to get better." And so I did; I was better for a time, sought some help a few years later when it got bad again, but mainly it was always the choice to get better that made the difference.

Did I suffer from mental illness? Yes. Was my salvation going to come from a pill? No. Our spirit, our soul, is much more powerful than a pill, and this applies to both sides of the equation. More than mental, I suffered from heartsick, spiritual illness.

After those years, I managed to find a way to live, yet still never knew happiness or a sense of well-being. I had no faith in anything and still lived with a silent death wish that hardly even felt like it was mine. It was just always there. I lived trying to avoid being depressed. I became numb. As long as I wasn't depressed and suicidal, I was doing well, or so I thought. I hadn't yet learned that true happiness was an option for me. I was dead inside, and even after my first big spiritual awakening, it wasn't until my heart fully awoke that I began fully living for the first time in this life. I was able to dig out the death wish and find a desire to live. Now, today, I embrace all of what makes me who I am. The same feelings that led me to depression led me to my dreams, my salvation, my soul, my purpose, greater wisdom, and real happiness.

"I know what it feels like," a statement that, for me, applies to all forms of inner suffering. I know what it feels like to have to force yourself to get out of bed, to brush your teeth, to eat, to do anything in life. I know what it feels like to live in hell, at the bottom, in fear, fear of yourself and the world, to be crippled by stress and anxiety, starved of love and anything good. To feel handicapped and alone, like you don't belong here, cut off from everyone, not understanding the social aspects of life. To barely be functioning, to be angry, to rage, to want to hurt or cut yourself, to be consumed with self-hate, to hate the sound of your own voice. To obsess, to feel crazy, to make yourself crazy... I created all of it, and it is for much of this that I am able to write this work. It was my path to awakening in this life, and I can barely begin to explain the gifts that were realized through it all, the metaphysical, spiritual gifts. I have within me the capacity for all flaws as well as all gifts. I prayed for God to take my life, but it turns out I was giving my life to God the entire time. My life has always belonged to all that is good. I now know what it feels like to touch heaven, to wake up happy for no reason at all, to repair the damage I did to my heart and soul, and to feel God with every cell of my being.

Many times it has felt like the entire universe shifted, and other times where the only word I could find for the feeling was God. Despite all the good that comes with an open heart, I still get nervous when I know it's coming, like being nervous coming face to face with God. Once the surrender happens, however, all gives way to unfathomable love and grace.

Emotional charge builds and releases in the process of spiritual growth. Today is a day to release. Depression has been lurking under the surface again, and it's time to let it go. To find joy, I must move through my heart. I must more deeply connect with the longing in my soul. My body too is prepared for what is to come with a final stretch toward the sky. Despite the slight tightness in my chest, my heart is engaged, and I'm ready to pour it into *the workout.* Symbolic of life, I will put all of my life into this birthday workout. I surrender myself to the vastness of it all.

Proceeding to the barbell, I load some plates and lift. Deadlifts, hang power cleans, and overhead presses flow set by set, one to another. The barbell feels right and good in my hands. A barbell is only off-balance if I'm off-balance, and as the barbell embraces the weight, so do I. I can easily spend an entire workout with nothing but a barbell and some plates. I push and pull, taking shorter and shorter rests between sets. Sweat drips down my forehead and neck as I nurture a *meditative state* *rests*. Intermittent spikes in heart rate and breathing help my chest continue to open, each moment getting closer to God. When I'm not sure I can do any more, I lighten the load and do more, and then move on to the next *lift*. Playing through my headphones attached to a tiny iPod is a careful selection of music – positive, upbeat, promoting strength and movement. The rhythm and words connect with my heart. Putting myself in the songs, each line becomes a mantra eliciting inner strength.

"Go hard! Or go home! Lord, use me! Lord, use me! Lord, use me! Lord, use me, Lord" raps the uplifting Christian artist, Lecrae, as I go as hard as I can, embodying this musical prayer.

A shift takes place. Gravity lets up, spirit lightens, and energy flows more freely. *The workout* takes flight with life of its own. Each *lift*, each set, has heart. I press the weight overhead and offer it up to God, holding it for as long as I can, until my entire body is temporarily fatigued. I continue to push until all of my heart is in *the workout*.

When the exertion stops, there is peace and calm as I stroll around the perimeter before returning to my special nook. I set my water beside the black mats, and sit. After a few moments of stretching and relaxing, opening my knees and hips, loosening tension in spots, I adjust into half lotus for a brief meditation. My spine is straight and slightly bowed, ready to tune in and receive. My eyes close. My brainwaves relax and slow to a deeper state. This is where it happens, what I knew was happening all along. This is where my heart bursts wide open, and again I can feel it all at once, only now it is overwhelming love, compassion, and gratitude for this life, for everything here on Earth and beyond. I sense an expansion of energy at the center of my chest. Waves of *enlightening emotions* arrive through the gateway of my heart. Cleansing tears well up as the presence of God flows through me. Conscious of still being in public, I control the valve, feeling freely while managing the outward expression. I allow tears to peacefully drop one or two at a time, going further into this beautiful human experience, simply feeling everything good, wholeheartedly, feeling God. Waves of love and gratitude continue to come from above, overwhelming gratitude simply for being alive.

I like to cry. I like to cry all different types of tears, and I want to feel as deeply as possible. This is when I am most happy, peaceful, joyous, and loving. This is what allows me to live freely. I cry for myself and I cry for the world. If I were a saint, perhaps I'd be the crying saint. It just feels good to cry, to let it all out, to know what matters, and to express my heart and soul.

With my heart now fully open and awake, there is nothing but a relaxed and clear vibration, a connection and soulful release. There is heart level, and then there is soul-heart level, when the heart and soul harmonize. The tightness in my chest is nowhere to be found; instead, a lightness of being accompanies this energy and vibration. This is why I do what I do, live how I live, and know what I know. I invite this soul connection and release, knowing each time I am growing spiritually, clearing root emotional charge and getting closer to the inevitable liberation of spirit, union with God, enlightenment – the end of suffering.

It is one thing to have these enlightening emotional experiences and another what we do with them in our lives. As a child,

I never knew what to do with these overwhelming feelings and lamentations. Like many others, I shut them off. I was afraid to feel. Now and in spiritual practice, this is what I ask for, to be humble and able to receive, for my heart to break so that light shines through, to see clearly through the eyes of God and love, and to see the beauty of the world in this light. In some ways, there is nothing better than feeling heartache and the love and compassion that accompanies it. You see, we can experience hurt without suffering. It is okay to hurt. We all as humans experience it. Our degree of denial is also the degree in which we deny ourselves of joy, happiness, and love. We appreciate life when we are near the end or experience loss. Someone with a death wish has a near-death experience and suddenly realizes the desire to live. Enlightening lessons and light shine through. In *the practice,* we learn to cultivate this power daily, for a life without heart is a life not fully alive.

Meditative fitness is heart, engaging, opening, and offering. *The practice* takes flight with heart, each workout an opportunity to do something significant for the benefit of one and all. Not all heartfelt workouts and meditations will look like the previous example; however, the important thing is for your heart to be engaged, which can be as simple as connecting with how you feel emotionally before, during, and after a workout or meditation. It can be as simple as connecting with why you're there in the first place, or as simple as pushing yourself physically. With heart, lean in to *the challenge*, enhance your performance, and maximize your growth in *the four key areas.* Without heart, your practice, performance, and growth are stifled and limited. Heart is emotion, energy, resolve, courage, love, character, understanding, humanity, centeredness, connecting to your truth, and so much more. Heart brings great presence, new levels of awareness, and maximizes intention and magnetism. You can reside in your head, your heart, or in union of the two. When your heart and mind align, you begin to experience your full potential. The heart has its own intelligence and opens the doors to higher intelligence. In spiritual practice, the heart is the gateway to the Divine, which can be directly experienced for yourself. Your heart helps you to go home within yourself and take your practice to deeper levels.

Many of us spend our lives building emotional charge without releasing it, without fully connecting with all that we are. Many of us have walls and guards around our hearts. Many of us do not fully express our hearts. We deny our feelings. Bottled charge negatively affects our state of being and potentially every moment of our lives. For example, compounding resentments eat at us from within to the point where even the slightest thing pushes a button, and our reaction doesn't match the situation. Suppressing emotion creates an imbalance in *the four key areas.* When disconnected from feeling, not consciously recognizing what is going on under the surface, we become more reactive and live a life of escape and avoidance. There are many ways we attempt to escape ourselves, the feelings residing underneath, the things we live with every day. These aspects of who we are have the greatest capacity for change and growth. They hold some of our greatest gifts. In facing what we are running from, we find our true strength and power.

In *meditative fitness*, we would like you to take a sledgehammer to those walls and lovingly obliterate them. Close your eyes and imagine taking a running start and blasting through your walls. However you want to take them down, just do it. Allow yourself to feel from a place of strength. Allow yourself to grow by feeling what you truly feel.

Deeply rooted feelings about ourselves and our lives creep into our behaviors and interactions with others, impacting our relationships and quality of life. If we deny ourselves of the lessons, we live on perpetual rerun, cyclical existence, over and over and over again. Getting stuck in a feeling happens when you hold on and carry the weight, refusing to release it. Feelings change and grow when you choose to move through them. No matter how scary it may be to feel some of what is in your heart, know that you will not get stuck in it if you continue to open and move through it, even if that means letting it gush out for an entire day, so long as it is productive and cleansing. To get unstuck, we surrender, move through our feelings, and do the heartfelt spiritual work to get to the other side.

Keep looking and keep asking. How much more of your heart is there to know? What feelings or past experiences pull the strings from deeper within? What are you avoiding or moving toward? What are you afraid of? What lights you up? What brings you joy?

Through *the practice,* we identify and transform these driving forces. We exchange any negative motivators for the guidance of inner light. We release negative emotional charge as often as needed and until we are at peace. Liberate yourself from the cycle.

Allow your heart to purify you from within. No more buttons for life to press; no more reactions, resistance, and attachment; no more liabilities – only freedom and gifts. The way you feel can and will change. Your spiritual life makes the difference between whether your heart feels like a burden or a blessing. Emotion can stem from ego or blossom from a soulful connection. The prayer is for the ego to give way to the soul, and when ego dissolves in the heart, we reach a soul-heart level connection.

Like other aspects of our growth, we are responsible for cultivating our own emotional intelligence. A lack of emotional maturity can lead to stress and anxiety, anger, rage, hatred, violence, strained relationships, drama, addiction, suicide, cutting, and broken families. Emotional intelligence means the ability to identify your feelings under the surface and allow yourself to feel them without causing harm to yourself or others. Emotional intelligence is taking ownership, acknowledging what you feel, and moving on better off because of it. Eliminate the notion of good or bad; it is simply the way you feel, the contents of your heart. This is the path of kindness and truth.

The heart knows. It adds another layer of consciousness and can provide instant answers without having to think. Like learning a foreign language, attuning the heart is a skill to develop in communication. You can speak or listen with heart. Heart recognizes heart, and heart recognizes truth. To speak from your heart, you must be present and connected to your truth based on where you are at the time. Heart and presence go hand in hand. Living with heart is about being real, true to what you feel, and true to what is real in the moment. It's about connecting with what is real to someone else. What are they feeling in your company and presence? When another is speaking from the heart, you can feel it, provided you are attuned and listening with an open heart. When you allow yourself to be vulnerable and share your heart, it is sacred ground. And when treated as such, our world becomes a better place, more open and heartfelt as a result.

With honesty, vulnerability, and surrender, the heart is where we connect (with ourselves and others), where we can go to never feel alone, where the lives of others live on after they pass, and where the teachings of Christ, Buddha, Krishna, and other spiritual masters come alive.

An open heart more deeply opens our intuition as a form of knowing. Sometimes faith is more than just faith. What is it that you know in your soul? Some truths remain constant throughout your life. The more you are aware of these lifelong intuitive truths, the more connected you are to your true nature. Do not ignore your intuitions. They might just save your life in more ways than one. Intuition provides foreshadowing when you are in danger, and it can also lead you to spiritual freedom. In your practice, you learn how to trust your intuition. You learn how to discern between true intuition and false doubts, worries, and fears. You can begin at any time by opening your heart. The intuitions are already there. It is here, right where you are, connected with heart, where intuition can be found.

What is it that you feel right now?

What do you feel? What is in your heart?

Look deeper. What do you really feel in there?

It is okay if you don't have immediate answers, but these are the questions to continue to ask yourself on an ongoing basis. Opening your heart and connecting to your truth can shift your entire world in an instant. This requires a deep surrender. When you close your eyes and allow your heart to release everything you feel, the world looks different when you open them. This can be so life-altering that you shift from seeing the world and everything in it as bad and wrong, to then seeing the beauty and perfection in all things. It can be so profound as to hear something different in your voice, to look in the mirror and see something different in your eyes, a different person staring back at you, yet someone you recognize. In the essence of change, this is the beginning of engaging the world differently, an often peaceful, serene, and strong feeling, as though you can approach and handle anything in your life.

Your heart is one of your greatest assets in *the workout*. Begin *the workout* with heart, surrender and embrace *the challenge,* and transcend your mind and body. Engage with your whole heart, and do more than go through the motions.

How powerful do you believe your heart to be? How much heart does it take to give all you have in your workouts? How much heart does it take to break through barriers, to continue when you don't think you can? What are you made of? The same raw materials as the stars. Awaken your heart to realize your power and potential during your workouts. Open the flood gates. Imagine the strength of a great waterfall or the rush of riding an enormous wave, embracing the momentum and energy. Your heart can fuel your workouts and provide the strength to go further than what you think is possible. Train as if your happiness depends on it, your life and fulfillment, for your practice can change your life and the quality thereof.

Meditative fitness is a heartfelt, humbling practice. Humility is needed to grow, and whenever we seek to grow, we can be graciously humbled by the process. Some try to resist being humbled by making excuses or creating false bravado. Insecure arrogance is a repellent combination. Humility requires courage, vulnerability, and truth, and is not to be confused with a lack of confidence. Humble confidence is a magnetic combination. Humbling activities are good for us, helping to create intimacy and bring us closer together. We are humbled in *the workout* by all the *skills, lifts,* and *movements.* We are humbled by the barbell and the weight, by the sensations and limitations of *the body.* We are humbled when we are gasping for air. We are humbled by *the challenge* and the soreness of our bodies afterward. We are humbled by someone stronger or better conditioned. We are humbled by our hearts.

When you witness someone following their dreams, training for something important to them, you see heart. When you see someone not giving up, getting back up after falling down, or finishing a race determined only to finish, you see heart and the resilience of continuing despite adversity. Your actions display your heart. What you do, how you engage your life, and how you treat others displays your heart. You see someone struggling and offer to lend a hand. You see someone fall and you help them up. You regard the feelings of others as equally important as your own. You are thoughtful, loving, considerate, and kind. You care. Even when you don't want to admit it, you care. You have heart.

The workout elicits heart, which can be found in a single *lift*, a set, or an overall workout. The more challenging *the workout*, the more heart is called upon, and the more emotion surfaces. What do we feel when we approach our first or 10th rope climb, when we hit failure halfway up the rope, when we hit failure in a workout only halfway through? What do we feel when we encounter something we can't yet do? *The challenge* calls on feelings under the surface to channel back into *the workout* and move through on an emotional level. Growth happens when you address the feelings you would like to transform, and when heart surfaces, it provides the perfect opportunity.

When something touches your heart in life, take advantage of the opportunity. When this happens, sit and close your eyes. Within moments you could be doing some deep inner work, releasing charge, connecting with the soul of who you are, aligning, and opening your eyes to love. Your heart begins to open. Something stirs within, pings your frequency. You examine closer with intention, presence, and awareness now in a heightened heartfelt state. Upon taking a closer look, it hits you. You know why it moves you, and you can feel the emotion welling from deep within. You recognize a significant aspect of who you are. You realize what matters to you. Now you have a choice. You can stuff it down, resist it, or perhaps feel it only a little. Or you can open the gates to all of it, surrendering and seeing what else is connected and where else it leads. Follow your heart and in a matter of a few moments, you may have new realizations and points of clarity as you clear emotional charge. Pay attention and observe any physical sensations. You may feel various vibrations in different areas of your body. You may feel the energy around your chest expand as you breathe more freely. You may feel lighter in spirit. You may feel more awake, for the energy of the heart awakens. Physically, an open heart dispels tiredness. Metaphysically, an open heart dispels fear, resentments, and surface-level emotions such as anger, irritability, stress, anxiety, and depression. This work helps us to be at peace and less reactive as we clear negative charge that has compounded throughout our lives.

To be willing and able to experience the depths of any emotion, to lean in to the contents of your heart, is standing strong in spirit – allowing yourself to feel is true strength and stepping into your power, owning that which you feel instead of everything else owning you. Once again, there is strength in vulnerability, especially in facing fear and hurt. Avoidance, escape, and stuffing our feelings align with inner weakness. We give away our strength by not allowing ourselves to feel, and we get stuck.

Meditative fitness helps to get us moving again. It is up to you to connect the string between your heart and mind, to connect with your heart and live more deeply, to touch bottom so you can rise.

Connect with what you feel and throw out any judgments. The way you feel is not always rational. Once again, it is simply the way you feel. It is your truth in the present moment, part of your experience and journey, and for this reason, there are no judgments. You are simply the observer of what you feel. Power and meaning are found in that truth, neither good nor bad, but a beautiful part of being human. Your feelings are not the problem; emotion provides feedback and guides you. Your reactions, resistance, habits, behaviors, judgments, and attachments in relation to the feelings present the problem. When you live with an open heart, you are less likely to suffer from a broken heart. It does not mean you won't experience hurt and feel heartbroken, but it doesn't have to be suffering. Hurt doesn't have to hurt. When connected to love and compassion, it means you care and that it matters. Offer the hurt to love, and the hurt becomes love. What you may not realize is that somewhere deep within you want to feel, to hurt, to experience, and for things to matter. Awareness tells you when you are attaching the pain and suffering to the hurt. You have the ability to wrap your heart around something without attachment. You can love and care and have compassion without making it a problem.

Deeper currents churn and impact surface weather, and the barometer of the heart provides constant feedback. Go under the surface of irritability, anger, stress, depression, and anxiety. If you ever get to a level of anger where you are ready to blow, about to do something you are not proud of, choose to slow down and pause. You don't have to do anything in that moment. Just stop. Stop everything, take a deep breath, and feel all of it, everything connected to the tip of the iceberg. Whether it's fear, hurt, losing control, unfulfilled desires, or other deep seated emotions, they are your true feelings under the anger, and they have nothing to do with anyone else but you. Filter the anger through your heart and continue breathing. Allow the turmoil to lead to peace. The choice is yours how long to stay in turmoil; perhaps you are not ready to grant yourself permission, or perhaps you are in a state of unworthiness, judging and punishing yourself, but the question is, how long is long enough for you?

Meditative fitness provides the opportunity for emotional success, moving forward and upward. Start from where you are, activate your heart, and offer it to *the workout*. Set your intention for how you want to feel. Wherever you are, however you feel prior to *the workout*, the work you put in helps get you where you want to be. Your physical effort is symbolic of your spiritual work. The greater the effort, the greater the credit toward your desired outcome. Do you believe you will reach your desired results if you don't put forth the effort? Action is directly related to what we believe possible. If we don't take action, we may never believe. If we have intention without action, constantly falling short, we run the risk of losing faith and trust in ourselves. Set yourself up for success with honesty. What can you do right now or today? What is your next small step?

In *the practice,* we run through emotions as we run through *the workout,* anything from insecurity, frustration, and disappointment to confidence, passion, and triumph. *Enlightening emotion* is productive, forward movement and growth, a healthy expression without judgment, wallowing, or self-created suffering. The heart we refer to in this chapter is very different than shallow, whining, self-pitying, hysterical, manipulative, or attention-seeking, unproductive emotion. We seek cleansing and freeing emotion. Much like you may feel something beautiful wash over you, you may feel something less-than-desired. Trust that something greater is always unfolding.

In the sports world we sometimes hear the notion of keeping your emotions in check. In *meditative fitness*, we would rather harness and channel emotional energy, using all of it, transforming detracting emotion into enlightening, performance-enhancing emotion. Opening your heart can help you to relax in tight moments and overcome nerves. We get nervous when something big is about to happen. Nerves mean it matters, that it is important to your heart. Channel the nerves through your heart and allow them to help you.

Connecting with your heart is about being honest with yourself.

How hard do you push yourself in your workouts?

How do you feel as you go through your workouts?

Motivated or lazy, energized or drained, embracing or resisting?

How much fun do you have?

How do you feel at the end of your workouts?

How do you want to feel?

Find what works for you and what lights you up inside. Have fun during your workouts. It can be so much fun to move *the body*. There are more options available for *the workout* now than ever before. What will bring you the most joy? Our number one job in life is to be happy. We are not here to suffer. *Meditative fitness* is intended to be a joyous engagement, and joy happens in the freedom of feeling what is in your heart. If you are stressed, there is a good chance you are storing stress within, storing the pressure and mounting charge. *The workout* can be a release so you can be free and at peace to move on. If you feel what you feel now, you can then begin to feel something different. Again, start from where you are, feel what you feel at a deeper level, and put it into the sacred space of *the workout.*

If there is music, let it in and allow it to flow through your heart. Let the music guide you. Music aligned with *the practice* promotes strength. Choose music that inspires, promotes movement, and elicits a strong inner response. Choose music with heart, a spiritual quality, or positive message, music that helps you take a look at yourself. Choose music that is uplifting, upbeat, waking parts of your being, inciting healthy passion and energy. Choose music that moves you and speaks to your soul.

Dancers learn to engage their hearts to maximize their presence and performance, connecting to and embodying the music. You may find yourself wanting to dance through your workouts. Embrace this, even if only tapping your foot to the beat. The way you hear the music tells you how open your heart is. Go for a meditative walk with some headphones on and dance your way down the sidewalk. See how it feels to be free. And then there is dancing without moving, feeling the music as energy and vibration, and allowing your soul to dance within. You can dance in your mind, dance in your heart, dance in your soul, and dance with your body. Physical dance, another form of *the workout,* is one of the most beautiful expressions of heart, mind, body, and soul.

Go as deep as possible, as often as needed, and soon you will be crying tears of joy. To laugh and cry at the same time is to experience all of life's beauty. How quickly we can go from deep sorrow to joy. It doesn't necessarily mean the sorrow is gone, but it means we can feel more than it may appear. In the freedom of vulnerable surrender, we are able to call upon all feelings, and one side can lead to the other. We may feel hate that leads to love, anger that leads to kindness, fear that leads to courage, and weakness that leads to strength. We find humility in order to connect with true confidence. We surrender to sorrow in order to find joy.

At the end of my soulful birthday workout, tears flowed on and off for over an hour, tears of spiritual growth, productive and cleansing, overcoming my challenges, releasing the depths of my soul, connecting more deeply with who I am. Upon leaving the gym, I allowed the floodgates to fully open and recorded a series of voice memos. With tears falling, I documented these sacred moments. In listening to them these many months later, they continue to move and awaken my heart. I share them here as an expression of my heart.

"Today is March 25th, and I'm ready to truly live. I am committed to this life, to health, to feeling good, to being happy and letting joy happen, and to do what I'm here to do. Love. There's no one I would rather be. I love this life. It's a good one. It's a really good one, and it's only getting better."

I never thought I would feel this way, perhaps why with each word, I was brought to my knees.

"This is my official birthday message. It has been quite a journey up to now. What do I want for my birthday? More than anything I want you and the world to know...there isn't anyone anywhere, man or animal, that I don't love and care about. I want you to be happy. I want you to be kind to one another even in the face of challenges, to slow down anytime you need to, to pause, simply to breathe and simply because you are alive.

"I've never met anyone I haven't wanted to be kind to, and the ones who challenge that are the ones I most want to be kind to, even if it's a kind dose of soul-shaking truth.

"I have always been one to ask, what's the point to all of this? And it used to be I was 'certain' there was no point. For years my only prayer was for God to take my life. I was disconnected and felt my soul dying. For me, now, the point is to be who I am, to love, to care, to be kind, to laugh and cry at the same time, to feel everything, including heartache, to help others find peace and happiness, and to continue to nurture this for myself, for without it, for me, there is no point. It is why I'm here. This is what I have dedicated my life to, what I will continue to dedicate my life to, and where I have known I was headed all along.

"I am so much looking forward to the rest of this journey that I must be careful not to get ahead of myself. There are many good things in store. I am happy even at times when it doesn't look like it. Most of all, I am happy to have the courage to be me."

May this book help awaken your heart and bring more peace, love, and joy to your life.

Processes for Reference

7

Energy

MY LOCAL GYM has a peaceful vibration on this early Sunday morning. I've been up for a couple of hours, yet can barely keep my puffy, cloudy eyes open. My long, slow blinks could easily turn into a deep sleep. My energy is heavy and weak, like a battery that has lost all charge. I didn't plan on working out today, nor do I really feel like it, but plans change, and I chose to take advantage of the opportunity to transform this sluggish energy. I knew if I didn't do something, I would be in for a long, tired day. Sometimes doing the opposite of what we feel like is exactly what is called for. In my debilitated state, I doubt my ability to really exert myself, but I'm going to anyway. *The workout* may be slow to start, but I vow to fully dedicate myself to *the practice.* I am determined to transform my energy and rise to this metaphysical test of ability.

It seems like a tall mountain to climb as I drag myself along. Last night, I treated myself to some chocolate ice cream. "Was it worth it?" I ask with each heavy and belabored step. Apparently I have an ice cream hangover and had been abstaining from sugar and dairy with good reason. Last night's indulgence, however delicious, has resulted in my present day muck, which is not how I desire to feel.

Inside the gym, I stagger to my nook and the cushioned mats. All I want to do is lie down and pass out. My water bottle hangs from my fingers, which I turn to for support. I'm thirsty; my insides feel strange and hot, as though water has gone to serve inflammation rather than aid the flow of energy. I twist the cap and take three big gulps of energy-flowing intention, easily the most refreshing liquid I've had in a while. You know that feeling, when water is perhaps the greatest thing to ever pass your lips, cooling you from the inside. I exchange the bottle for a wooden staff that leans against the corner, similar to a tool used at the Den for mobilizing, stretching, and teaching *lifts*. I am grateful for the one here, likely brought in by one of the trainers. Ever since I was a child, wielding a wooden staff instantly transforms me into an imaginary martial artist. With straight arms, a wide grip, and the staff resting at my waist, I raise it from my hips to my behind, creating an arc over my head, going back and forth, then progressing to rotating one direction, then the other, with the stick dancing around my body and my arms traveling in opposite directions.

My heart pumps more readily. Blood flows through the heavy energy, pulsating throughout my body, throbbing, which is a common indication of *the body* reacting to food or some other stimulus. With my feet planted, I squeeze to activate my legs and glutes. I take a deep breath until no more air can enter, and I focus on opening my energy centers, expanding my chest and diaphragm. I squat down with the staff parallel to the ground, cradled by my thumbs with my hands together, prayer-like. My elbows press out against the inside of my knees. I lean to one side, then the other, with my weight resting on one foot at a time, stretching each ankle and calf. I've witnessed J.D. teach this many times while squatting next to him. Yogis might refer to this as a version of crow pose, and mobility master Kelly Starrett has the "10-Minute Squat Test." Here we refer to it as a meditative squat.* Whenever we hold a position such as hanging from a high bar, holding a barbell, a handstand, a yoga posture, or sitting with a straight spine, it is meditative in nature as we focus our will and energy.

Regardless of whether I sit in meditation, I work with my energy daily, standing, stretching, or moving my body – a breath here, a breath there, a release, a grounding, flowing energy up, clearing, lifting, relaxing, and being at peace.

After a few breaths in the squat, I stand up, close my eyes, and continue to tune in to my body so that I can assist the flow, sending oxygen and energy with each breath to every cell. I relax the tension I am carrying in my face and shoulders. I shake out my legs, hips, and arms, and begin to bounce up and down as relaxed as possible. At first, these are heavy bounces, but that doesn't stop me. The bounce turns into a process of becoming lighter.* I start to shuffle side to side, floating back and forth on the balls of my feet while staying in place. My intention is for my energy to lighten as I move. I am meditating in motion and lightening with each breath, imagining light energy replacing heavy, and it's working. I feel distinctively lighter, both in spirit and on my feet. Upon stopping, my energy has risen and is flowing much better, but still not all the way there, still with a sense of weakness. When

I make a fist, my grip feels weak and signals the same to the rest of my body. I reach down for my water bottle, repeat the intention-filled prayer, and chug down more energizing gulps. Water will continue to aid the river of energy.

Prior to entering *the workout*, it is important for our energy to be flowing freely. The physical warm-up and hydration serve this purpose, getting our blood flowing and lubricating joints and muscles. And we can complement this with meditation – practicing being light in spirit, opening our heart, lungs, and the energy centers of our body. We all exude an overall life-force, and we also possess separate, yet connected, energy centers throughout *the body*. These are also known as chakras, of which the seven primary run from the base of your spine to the top of your head. More than a physical sense, it may help to think of these as the reason why we can feel a certain energy in a particular area, and why we are able to clear and open that area. If my chest is tight, I open my heart. If my head is cloudy, I open and clear that space. Energy flows when we are open. It flows when we move our bodies, when we heighten our mental resolve, and when we flip an inner switch, wake up, or have new realizations.

With the warm-up complete, I enter the field of *the workout* arena. Two light plates are loaded onto a barbell. Sitting on an incline bench underneath the bar, I close my eyes, breathe, and *anchor* to strength. My left hand represents the intention of strength. My right hand represents the weak energy I am experiencing. My hands come together with the weak energy collapsing into strength. Lying back, I reach up to grip the bar. My spine arches naturally as I set my shoulders and lats, creating tension and torque for the *lift*. The bar comes easily off the rack, but feels awfully heavy for such a light load. I lower it to my chest and press it back up eight times before carefully placing it back on the rack. Sitting up, I close my eyes and again summon strength and energy, flowing and spinning the weak energy up in exchange. I turn to my water with the same intention. The second set feels heavy again for eight more reps. I sit up and close my eyes for the third time, when, in an instant, the energy changes. Strength returns like a vibration of atoms and molecules arriving, like a mist of strength particles washing over me. I test by tightening my now strong fist, which sends the signal to the rest of my body, as if to say, "Here...we...go."

"Wow, that water is really kickin' in," I joke to myself.

With no coincidence, a powerful song streams through my headphones and further infuses me with the strength of higher purpose and a higher power. Intentions and prayers are answered with energy.

"I'm back," I say inside with increased will and determination to work for a higher cause. More weight is added to the bar, but it now feels lighter in my hands. I complete the set with ease.

"Wow...what a difference. Okay, okay, let's see how far we can take this." Enough weight is added to make it a personal record. The barbell feels solid in my hands for a new three-rep max. Five more pounds are added, and three more reps are completed for another new personal record. Five more pounds. Three more reps. Another PR.

"Okay, I'm a believer. What's next?" I laugh, ready to raise the bar.

I walk with purpose to the pull-up bar, and for the next 12 minutes, I alternate between burpee pull-ups and 300-meter rows. Exhilaration ensues in flying from the air to facedown on the ground and back in the air all in a matter of seconds. I practice doing so as lightly and gracefully as possible, both expending and conserving energy. It brings me joy to practice catching the bar without looking, to be breathing hard and releasing energy. It brings me joy to find the rhythm of the row while beautiful artists sing in my ears. With as much energy as ever before, I entered a *meditative fitness* zone in those 12 minutes.

In general, and specifically that day in the gym, I am consistently amused and surprised at what is possible. It is not that I didn't believe in the possibility, for I most certainly believed. Otherwise, I wouldn't have bothered to leave home. It is only that there are no guarantees. Some days, energy has been miraculously transformed, and other days, tired and weak energy has lingered after futile attempts to change it. I previously thought that day might be one of the latter, however, because of *the practice,* it was a day for so much more.

Meditative fitness is energy, connecting, flowing, and rising. In *the practice,* we give our energy with intention, presence, and awareness. We give our energy with our thoughts, heart, breath, body, and vision. There are many different forms of energy. Like awareness, energy is all encompassing, the essence of our being, and always present. There is no such thing as a "lack of energy." Instead, we experience the energy present in the moment, and we always have access to clear, awake energy. Your job is to observe your spiritual life (happiness, inner world, lightness or heaviness of being) and work with your energy. Make choices to transform your energy, and create a positive upward flow.

With presence, our energy is grounded. If we find ourselves spaced out, we bring our energy back into presence, back within ourselves. We give our energy to the present moment. Our thoughts, intention, heart, and vision all help magnify and direct our energy. Our breath and our bodies help us to connect with and conduct our energy, and *the workout* is an act of energy expenditure, management, and replenishment.

Heart and emotion, a powerful form of energy, can be felt, cleared, and exchanged as raw energy, transforming from heavy to light, dull to vibrant, weak to strong, tired to awake, anxious to relaxed, from sorrowful to joyful, and from unhappy to happy. Heart magnifies energy and changes the vibration. When you speak, chant, sing, or hum, practice feeling like the vibration is coming from your heart. Place your hand over the center of your chest to help sense this.

Connecting with your energy happens easiest when you close your eyes and sit or stand completely still, focusing on your breath. You have the ability to work with your energy – to clear, release, exchange, direct, focus, and transform your energy. You likely already do this to some degree in your life. This work, by making it more conscious, helps you create a consistently higher vibration.

If you focus on everything outside of yourself, you may find your energy limited and easily drained. As a practice, rather than spilling or spewing energy outward everywhere you go in the form of thoughts, words, and actions, rather than giving all of your energy to the endless void of material or external desires, first withdraw your energy inward and direct it upward, then allow it to flow back through you to your world. This is the same as finding happiness within rather than looking for it everywhere outside of yourself. This is the same as putting your spiritual life first, putting God first, which many would like to do but may not know how on an ongoing basis. Energy is the how, by consciously or "physically" flowing our energy inward and upward, then allowing God to flow back through us into our lives. This is the path of unlimited energy, Divine inspiration, and how we are able to do the most good in the world.

Energy – the vibration of molecules, invisible to the naked eye – resides in all things and provides another perfect intersection of science and spirituality. Everything radiates energy and can be perceived with its own unique vibration, which can also change with the potential to evolve and expand or shrink and decay. There is the energy of a room, a space, a building, a mountain, and even a simple rock. There is the unique energy of a town, a city, a person, a creature, or a flower. There is the energy of a song, a dance, a *lift*, or a *movement*. There is the vibration of this book and the words on this page. Everything has an essence of being.

This book captures the metaphysical nature between meditation and fitness. The essence is what matters, the meaning, the vibration, the energy. This is the same as when someone uses the wrong word, but you still know what they mean. We may not always have the "right words," but we do our best to convey the right meaning. With practice, learn to detect and perceive the essence of things and be sensitive to the vibration of others. The essence is where universal truth is found in all the great religions and teachings of spiritual masters. No need to look for the falsehoods. No need to look for the argument. Look for the truth in all things and all religions, and you shall find it. Look for understanding as a form of agreement.

When we understand and see this connection to the energy of all things, our intuition and consciousness rise to a new level. We sense another dimension, at times wondering how it is we know what we know. Hardly able to explain it, we understand the unexplainable.

Within moments of contact with someone, you can read and sense their energy. Whether calm, anxious, or anywhere in between, you can sense their vibration, the frequency they are transmitting in the moment. This reading has the potential to convey the most about a person, including their karma – and it happens in an instant. One question to ask is, "What energy do I feel in relation to this person?" Granted, this is by no means solely about the other person, for they too are a mirror into yourself, and it is very easy to misinterpret or see through your own set of filters that cloud this sense. But those would be the next questions to ask yourself as you do your own energy-check: "Is the energy I am sensing created by me? Am I triggering it or contributing to it? Or am I falsely perceiving due to what is going on inside of me?"

Either way, your sense is a moment in time. You may gain much insight into a person; however, it is not the be-all and end-all. It is not a judgment or finality. It is simply your intuitive perception and observation in the moment.

At times we may find ourselves overly concerned with the energy of others, but we must return to the universal truth of continuing to look at ourselves and take care of our own energy. You make the difference in your experience and what you draw or magnetize from others. When you cross paths with someone whose energy is upsetting, awareness of your own energy is critical to avoid getting sucked into this attractor. Otherwise, you may find yourself acting the very way you are upset about in another, meeting rudeness with rudeness or anger with anger. Instead, observe yourself and seek to be faithful to your true nature.

What is your predominant energy in life?

What do you radiate?

Anxious, impatient, frantic, flighty, fearful, worrisome, irritable, angry, arrogant, insecure, sad, tired, or calm, peaceful, clear, confident, loving, kind, pure, authentic, passionate, vibrant, full of life. Again, no matter what, you can change and raise your vibration, and your practice can help you accomplish that feat whenever needed.

You are responsible for fanning your own flame. As a guide, follow the path to increased energy. Do things that light you up inside. There are two paths. Our choices and actions either increase our energy and align with strength or drain our energy and align with weakness. Sometimes this means we have to make difficult decisions. Others can greatly impact our energy, and in turn, we can greatly impact the energy of others. We are connected. We continuously exchange energy. Whether disheartened or inspired, we live in this world together and can't help but be influenced by each other. Our energy is contagious and makes a difference. In spiritual and fitness communities, in the company of others with similar higher purpose, engaging in meditation or *the workout* together, the energy is exponentially multiplied.

Transforming your energy can be as simple as opening your heart or taking a series of deep breaths. With each inhale, gather the undesired energy and emotion, all that is going on inside of you. Release with each exhale, allowing the energy to flow up and out from wherever it is felt. As a variation, spin the energy up and out like a little funnel leaving your body. Next, practice an exchange, breathing clear life-giving energy until you are overflowing with it. In raising your vibration, you will correspondingly raise the vibration of your surroundings.

As you develop your energy awareness, it will become easier to tap into this realm and flow with the energy of the Universe. When you find yourself stuck, swimming upstream, meeting resistance, or trying to force your way through life, ask what you can do to step back in the flow.

How light or heavy do you feel? How light or heavy is your energy in this moment? How light or heavy do you feel throughout your life? Your answers to these questions illuminate how healthy you are in spirit, and this is your spiritual life.

You may encounter days when you feel weak, tired, or heavy, with lower energy and a lower vibration. Regardless of the reason, these days are your greatest opportunities to change and transform your energy, going from where you are to where you want to be, rising from a lower state to one of strength and vibrant energy.

To help determine the reasons for lower energy, examine the following: Food – are you lacking fuel or is your body reacting to poor nutrition? Hydration – have you been drinking enough water? Sleep – are you lacking quality sleep or suffering from irregular sleep patterns? Training – are you recovering well enough in relation to the intensity of your training? Or is it mental, emotional, and spiritual? Know that whatever is zapping your energy can be cleared and resolved, and you can recharge in very little time.

If you ever experience puffy eyes or a cloudy, foggy mind, this can also be related to food, water intake, sodium, sleep, digestion, inflammation, or water retention. At the same time, the puffiness is the energy in and around the eyes, similar to knots or trigger points in muscle tissue. These are examples of clogged or cloudy energy. If you *go in* and work on clearing and releasing these pockets, energy begins to flow and you rid yourself of the puffiness, cloudiness, or tightness. The clogged energy dissipates, and you will feel more alert and awake with your eyes clear and open as a result. Energy clearing* such as this can be powerful for your workouts, and there are many different techniques that you can practice.

Imagine giving all of your energy and still feeling more awake at the end of a life-changing workout or meditation. *The workout* can be energizing, creating a tremendous flow of energy. Your job is to help manifest this energy. *The workout* doesn't have to deplete your energy and make you tired. Instead, give while receiving from the infinite energy of the Universe. Deepen and heighten your practice, and allow *the workout* to help wake you up.

The body requires energy to move. When we run, we manifest and expend energy. If we want to move a heavy weight or execute a challenging *movement*, we must gather that kind of energy, aligning with intention in mind and body, putting ourselves in an energy of strength. The barbell, weights, *movements*, and facility help trigger strength within ourselves. We approach a *lift* from a place of strength and intention that the weight is going to move. We gather energy and send it through our muscles. We engage explosive energy, and when we hit a wall, we must recover and summon more energy to keep going.

Both fitness and meditation help us tap into this energy realm. Both help awaken the flow of energy along the spine as well as awaken us to the sensation of energy flowing throughout *the body*. In the sport of fitness, your performance depends on your ability to manage and recover your energy. At a high intensity, completing the next rep and the overall workout can depend on how quickly you can clear fatigue. Sometimes, even a split second of rest on a *movement* is enough to help you keep going and better perform in a timed workout.

One of the greatest benefits of *meditative fitness* for performance is better management of energy, efficiently expending all available energy, emptying the tank, and recovering more quickly. Remember, rest and recovery moments are meditative moments. Performance improves with energizing breaths, thoughts, and heart. Learn how to work with your energy in meditation and take it with you into your workouts. Learn what works for you to quickly recapture and recharge your energy pathways.

In any timed workout, your results depend on how well you manage your energy. With efficient *movements*, you expend the least amount of energy as possible to maximize the number of repetitions. Once familiar with your energy in relation to specific *movements*, you intuitively know how to navigate a workout. If you come out explosively and burn all of your energy-meter, you will have a difficult time continuing at a decent pace. Different-length runs provide a simple example. You govern yourself so that by the end, your energy-meter is completely, yet temporarily, depleted.

As stated previously, we already do much of this energy work inherently, and the processes following these chapters will help hone these natural abilities. In *the practice,* we enhance these capabilities so we can tap into all of our potential in life and in *the workout.*

Returning home from my energizing workout, I had much more passion than when I departed. As I sat down and prepared to write, I opened a newly arrived voice memo and pressed "play." I heard Scott's voice beaming, "The flow of energy and connectedness in *the workout*..."

Hearing his peaceful voice brought a smile and something similar to chills, like God telling me to pay attention. Scott continues, "Energy in *the workout* comes from all that surrounds you! From other athletes, from the vibration of the box, from the natural world outside. Tuning in to deeper harmony allows greater energy to power *the workout*! We learn connectedness, flowing with instead of working against. Nothing is working against you. We are not competing against, but rather competing alongside everyone. If your energy is going with your opponents or the clock or whatever you are doing, your strength is increased because you are flowing and working together. Most importantly, connect to your faith in your workouts and you will have an infinite source of strength!"

"Perfect," I think to myself with a big smile on my face and in my being, breathing and radiating peaceful, joyous energy.

Processes for Reference

8

The Breath

No time to waste with the barbell on my back. As if preparing to plunge under water, I took a big gulp of air before plunging into a heavy squat, then rising with a powerful exhale, coming up for another breath before plunging under again. Each set was a mini-meditation.

Standing on the platform, I paused to breathe for a moment before attempting my first successful "heavy" clean. The barbell needed to travel from the ground to above my waist before I was to pull myself underneath it to catch it on my shoulders in a deep squat. Months of practice and drills led up to these attempts. Many times I lifted this weight and was afraid to jump under the bar, but on this day, I jumped and missed three times. Fear was creating reservations in my movement, but I first needed to learn I could miss safely in order to break through the barrier. As I stood there breathing, I relaxed and found courage within myself, visualizing success through the rhythm of the *movement*. Then I stepped up to the bar, stepped through the barrier, and set a new clean and jerk personal record.

My eyes are closed as I reminisce about these breaths. Elevated a foot-and-a-half off the ground by a pair of upside-down crates, my bottom rests toward the front of the top cushion with my legs crossed in half lotus beneath me. This became my favorite place to sit from the moment I constructed it. You may find yourself drawn to certain spaces to conduct your practice. You may feel the need to make little adjustments to your surroundings to bring the right energy to a space, which also changes alongside yourself through a nice meditation. Good spaces to sit or stand can be found anywhere. To lead a meditative life, wherever you are, the space you occupy, is the perfect space.

I breathe in and feel an inner expansion, pausing slightly at the top, and releasing with a wave of relaxation washing over me. Ah, to breathe – simply to breathe – is a beautiful thing. One breath is all it takes to be at peace, and one fulfilling breath follows another as I relax and go home within myself. With every enlightening breath I take in this life, I move closer to God and pure being. Inhales and exhales come and go as I sit and enjoy the rise and fall, pulling up images of *the breath* from prior workouts.

I recently returned to Tiger's Den after a long absence for a special workout called "Hope." The word alone means a lot to me, having eluded me for too long in prior days before giving me new life upon its arrival. Because of my journey, I have at times been able to offer and give hope to those most hopeless, to go into the darkness and shine light, to fight on behalf of another's soul and happiness. This has been my life's work since long before this life. This is the work of my soul. If anyone reading this needs hope in any capacity, you can borrow some of mine. Whatever it is, it can get better. Hope is the first step in believing something different is possible. I believe it is possible. I have hope for you. All it takes is one ray of light, and hope can arrive in a single breath. Surrender, allow your heart to open, and allow hope to flood in. I have hope for you. It all starts getting better right now. From here, the only direction you are going is up. There is hope for all of us.

Scott and I met early again like we did on our first occasion, almost one year after that fateful workout, of which "Hope" is the same format – three rounds of five minutes, one minute per exercise, with one minute of rest between rounds. In previous training at the Den, after only my first few workouts, I noticed vast improvement in lung capacity and endurance. The chemistry of my body changed, and the sensations during intense exertion weren't such a shock.

"Hope" was a test of many breaths, the entire workout a series and pattern. Prior to the start, anchored in my breath, I abided by an athlete's intuition and practiced entering an ideal state of relaxed readiness, gathering strength while creating a lightness of being. In the first minute, I paced myself for as many smooth burpee breaths as possible, in and out and in again for each time my chest touched the ground. It took very little time for me to be breathing quite hard, the clock ticking with each breath.

My breath helped stabilize my core and midline in the power snatches, a *lift* where you take a wide grip on the barbell and stand to launch it straight overhead. When my face, chest, shoulders and arms tightened, when no area of my body was getting enough oxygen, my breath helped loosen the tightness, filtering from my face to everywhere else as my breathing returned to a smooth pace.

Relaxation flows with *the breath*, and the pattern was written for me to relax whenever tightness appears. We have a tendency to make all kinds of twisted faces at maximum output, and tension in our faces typically means tension in other areas. The face is an easy area to relax and help spread relaxation. Tightness tends to mean short, shallow, upper chest breaths, inefficiently spinning our wheels. In *meditative fitness,* we practice smooth and efficient delivery of oxygen and energy to *the body*, especially at a high intensity. This is *the practice,* and every breath matters.

Spectators from other heats cheered us on. Sometimes all it requires is for us to hear someone say, "Come on, let's go!" Other times, it requires us to say it from within. I reached down to put my hands back on the bar as a small commitment to continue working. *The workout* didn't allow for enough time to fully catch your breath. Every second and every breath counted. The bar flew from the ground with a powerful exhale and skimmed across my body until caught overhead, arms open wide as if embracing the world. Five fierce breaths equaled five power snatches. Two relaxing breaths equaled enough rest to return to the bar again.

For the box jumps, I exhaled with a short burst while simultaneously leaving the ground, completing as many as I could with my lungs fully burning, redlining, breathing as hard and fast as my lungs would allow. By the second round, sweat, drool, and snot ran together, wafting off my mouth with strong gusts of exhalations. Breathing and completing the next rep was more important than any of that. "Normal" no longer applied in that place of maximum RPM's.

Disoriented, I walked toward the pull-up bar before realizing it was time for the thrusters. With my breath, I regrouped, refocused, and quickly recovered before going to work on this challenging *lift* that involves a front squat followed by a thrusting overhead press. A moment later, I found the rhythm for thrusters, *the breath* to match the *movement*. They called for a *core breath* while descending in the squat before releasing it on the drive up and overhead. It didn't take long to realize how hard they were. Breathe, squat, press, breathe, squat, press, breathe, squat, press, hit a wall, drop the bar, rest, breathe, breathe, breathe, relax, and back to the bar.

In between sets of chest-to-bar pull-ups, I could be seen bending over with my back straight and my hands on my knees, working to regain my breath and composure. Bending over is one thing, but collapsing my spine and diaphragm is not something I am willing to do, not in meditation or *the workout.* All I could do and all I wanted to do was breathe. I was breathing so hard I heard a muffled static in my ears before lifting myself up and expanding my chest to create as much room for my breath as possible. Nothing opens the chest quite like the equivalent of sprinting in these short bursts.

"Rest! One minute," yelled Collin at the end of the second round as I walked around in a daze before catching my breath again. I looked over to see Scott sitting on his plyo-box, also breathing at full capacity, with a priceless look of *the workout* on his face, of giving himself to the moment. I wish I could have captured that image. *The workout* is an act of giving, and Scott is a very giving soul. There was vulnerability in those moments of maximum effort with hearts and souls on display. He was in his own meditative world, and I returned to mine, breathing and steadily recovering. The one minute of *rest* went by too quickly before the last five minutes of onslaught arrived, and the breaths continued. We gave *the workout* every breath we had. We found peace in the exertion and light in the form of the finish line. We continued to move toward the light with each breath, and nothing felt better than the calm breaths that followed this level of output.

After recounting my breaths with "Hope," I open my eyes. Still sitting on my cushion, I bring my mind back to the sensation of air passing my lips, rising from my throat, chest, and diaphragm. The regular question to ask oneself is, "What does my breathing feel like?" This takes no time as an awareness. We feel *the breath*, test it, and test the energy related to it in that moment. How clear and open is the energy from your throat down to your belly? Still early, my chest and lungs are not yet fully open and awake. With a little stretching, expansive breathing, energy meditation, and physical activity, this will be quick to change. I lean back and arch my spine, pushing my upper torso up and out, stretching the muscles and opening my chest. With a deep breath, I expand from within, feeling the air push against my body on the inside. My stomach is relatively empty other than some fluids, allowing for plenty of room for *the breath*. I practice starting each inhale and exhale from my belly. Anything I do now, training my breath, will help the meditation of *the workout*.

I hear the air softly whistle through my nose as it fills my lungs. On the exhale, I hear a variety of gentle sounds as the air passes my throat and lips, each passage having their own sound and sensation. An individual's fingerprint can be found in the sounds and characteristics of their unique breath. I tend to subtly accentuate sounds to go along with different intentions, creating multi-sensation *anchors* with my breathing.

Sitting, observing, and receiving, the many aspects of breathing flow through: inhale, exhale; nose, mouth; speed, strength, force; capacity, length, duration, pace, rhythm, repetition; sound, sensation, and depth. We can take one long breath per minute or one quick breath per second, shallow from our chest or deeper from our diaphragm, smooth and easy or strong and powerful. With no manipulation, the natural breath has a natural rise and fall. And then there are conscious, overriding, intention-filled breaths, and any combination of inhales and exhales – a quick or a slow rise and fall, in through the nose or mouth and out through the nose or mouth, and breaths where the throat is more open or closed. Each type of breath has its own sensations, and in any moment, you can automatically go to the specific breath that best serves your intention. Life, meditation, and *the workout* are a series of breaths. A meditation can be spent focusing on one type of breath or a combination of different breaths, and *the workout* has breaths to match every *movement, skill,* and *lift.*

With one breath, we connect with our flow of energy. With one breath,* we relax and melt away stress and anxiety. With one breath, we gather strength or exert power. With one breath, we surrender to our hearts. With one breath, we sing, speak, or cry out. With one breath, we enter the world, and with one breath, we depart this life. With one breath, we connect with all that we are.

Meditative fitness is *the breath,* working with and becoming, each breath an opportunity. Master your breath, and you can master energy and your body. Master your breath, and you can master *lifts, movements,* and *the workout.* As part of *the foundation, the breath* threads it all together. If you simply learn to connect with your breath and relax, you can do many things. Nearly everything you do in meditation, you can do in union with your breath. Connecting it with intention, you can open your heart, flow with energy, expand awareness, and bring yourself into greater presence. *The breath* is the wind in the sails of spirit and *the body.* In *meditative fitness,* we seek to exercise control over our breath, to expand lung capacity, to access unseen resources, and to reach our highest potential in harnessing the energy that comes with *the breath.* Your breath is how you allow the opportunity of every moment to be part of your practice. We may not always make time for meditation, but we always have time to breathe.

If you take quick and shallow breaths, you are likely to feel tight and anxious. If you breathe deeply with a long exhale, you are likely to relax and find more peace. If you breathe powerfully, you are likely to feel strong.

Our physical and spiritual lives are tied to *the breath*. Anyone who has had difficulty breathing for any reason knows how crippling it can be. Great suffering and a closed heart are often accompanied by a tightness in your chest, like having the weight of the world on you. But when you surrender to your heart and release the energy, when the weight is lifted, you can take a deep, soothing, peaceful breath again.

As a conduit for inner change, with your breath, you learn to ground, relax, create strength and peace, magnify your energy, and so much more. Your practice is where you learn these techniques for yourself and find what works for you, and the processes following these chapters are there to help. With belief, initiative, and creativity, you will find yourself doing things you never realized you could do. It is one thing to read and learn about these things and another to experience them. My continual prayer is that you will experience much of this material in your practice, in your own way. And you can start with one breath.

Follow your breath, observe the rise and fall, and become *the breath.** For the most ancient and fundamental of meditations, and to help quiet the mind, whenever you find your mind racing, simply bring yourself back to your breath, and with a deep inhale, slowly let it fall and observe, paying attention to the presence of sensations. Add another layer, and along with your breath, bring yourself back to repeating a silent intention or vision. What will you create with your breath?

Close your eyes and follow one breath after another. See if you can determine where your breath ends and where you begin. This is an exercise of connection and leads to what it feels like to be one with all, oneness of breath and being. Once again, the essence of the experience, rather than the words and names for things, is what matters.

As part of the parasympathetic nervous system, the lungs function and breathing happens whether we focus on it or not. In meditation, we drop into a parasympathetic state and add intention to our breathing. We train *the breath* as an instrument. *The breath* can be the difference-maker for executing an intention in meditation or a successful *lift* in *the workout.* Once grounded in your breath, each moment contains enhanced possibilities, and your breath can be one of your greatest strengths.

In *the workout,* we exercise our lungs as conductors of oxygen and energy, impacting every cell in our bodies. We open our lungs along with our heart, throat, and other energy centers. We expand lung capacity and create oxygenating benefits throughout *the body.* We gather strength with our breath, and we unleash it with an explosive exhale. We grunt powerfully, breathing strength into the movement of weight. Think about trying to execute a heavy *lift* with a weak, whimpering breath. It is simply not going to happen. *The breath* is strength. Your breath represents your force, power, and energy. Imagine taking a deep breath in, and with a powerful exhale, you are able to move a large brick wall. Imagine applying that degree of strength and intention in a challenging *lift.* Imagine taking a deep breath in and as you exhale, with the help of your arms, hands, and body, you unleash all the strength within you...WHOOSH!*

With a *core breath*, we stabilize our core in *lifts,* and with a *core breath*, we breathe deeply at the core of being. Sitting up straight, starting in your belly, draw a breath in and feel the air push your belly out from within. Expand this to your chest and take in as much air as possible. When it doesn't feel as though you can take in any more, expand a little more, all the way up to your throat. Place your hand over your belly to help make the connection. On the exhale, release and allow the air to flow out, and when you don't think you can exhale any more, contract and push out every last bit of air. That is one rep exercising full lung capacity. The inhale and exhale are equally important in developing and strengthening your breathing. Try 20 reps in meditation for the purpose of expanding your lung capacity as well as building new neural connections.

Some *movements,* such as carrying heavy objects, may only allow for a core stabilizing breath followed by quick, short breaths as the *movement* is executed. In any sustained physical exertion, you can find rhythm with your breath. Each *lift* and *movement* has its own rhythm. At maximum effort, we complete as many reps as possible, then recover before going at it again. As in a timed workout, chipping away at repetitions, performing well is often about finding a process. Once you find your process for the given situation, you repeat the types of breaths, durations of time, and number of breaths the reps and recovery require.

In high-intensity fitness, your breathing represents your rotations per minute and is one of the keys to peak performance. When you lose your breath, you lose everything else. Without proper breathing, your muscles fail in a heavy *lift,* and when you feel as though you cannot breathe, you must pause to rest. Performance suffers as measured by less physical output over time, but this is also your rising level of fitness, conditioning, and your ability to handle anything and recover quickly.

While meditation isn't a performance, your breathing makes a difference in the experience and in your results. Meditation suffers when your breath is strained and when your energy centers are clogged or foggy. This could be related to mental or emotional health, a closed or shut-down heart, dehydration, tight muscles, or reactions to food and digestion. Symptoms include an inability to focus, tired or weak energy, distracting physical discomfort, and a variety of other *abnormalities.* At times, each breath may make you want to yawn, which you can then use to help release the energy. An entire meditation can be spent clearing this to get back up to the ground floor and beyond. It is all part of your practice with your breath.

You never know where your breaths will take you. When J.D. and I met recently to discuss the book, we spontaneously found ourselves at the grand opening of a Lululemon store, a brand popular to fitness and yoga practitioners alike. We ventured outside and around the corner to behold a large mobile unit with images of athletes and the words "CRYOUSA, Athletic Recovery

Center" and "MAXIMUM EFFORT REQUIRES MAXIMUM RECOVERY," all surrounded by an emanating icy glow.

"I couldn't agree more," I thought to myself as we put ourselves in line for a whole-body cryotherapy session. Cryotherapy is a recovery method that uses a blast of extremely cold temperatures to trigger healing and reduce inflammation. This was something we needed to try.

As we waited, from a big-screen TV, I learned that the chamber basically freezes your entire body for up to three minutes and has a host of benefits. The wait alone was exhilarating, thinking about stepping into negative-220 degrees Fahrenheit. When I was on deck, I was directed to a small restroom to put on a robe. Moments later, I walked through the door and down a couple of steps to behold a large, silver, cylindrical spaceship-looking apparatus. Clearly, this could have been a scene from a science fiction movie of decades past. I was guided by a man with a genuine, friendly vibration, part of a greater community of athletes. After I put on some slippers and gloves and confirmed I still had my underwear on (all important considerations), he had me step onto the inner platform of the chamber and closed the door behind me.

"Ready or not, here we go," I thought. The chamber began circulating the same icy glow as the images outside.

"Ooh, ah, woooow!" Within seconds I was engulfed by icy fog. My skin felt like every receptor was turned on, colder than ice, wrapped in a frozen blanket. The only warmth left was within myself. Being the middle of summer in Texas, the contrast of going from 100 plus degrees to minus 220 is difficult to describe. Slowly and carefully, I began to turn in circles as instructed. My entire body began to shiver. I flashed back to one of my earliest childhood practices from before I was conscious of meditation in this life. I used to go out in the cold and practice overcoming the shivers with the power of my mind. "Mind over body," I would say to myself while taking smooth breaths, warming from within. Perhaps it was then when I began to learn the importance of *the breath*.

"How you doin' in there? You okay?" asked the cryo man. He surely noticed the chattering teeth and shivering head sticking out.

Even if it wasn't visible on my frozen face, I was smiling on the inside. Time, however, like my cold body, was nearly frozen in those minutes.

"Gooood. It's aaalll about-t-t *the b-b-breath-h*," I drew out through chattering teeth before attempting the smoothest, most relaxing, warmest breath I could muster. The shivering calmed ever so slightly. Enjoying every second of this opportunity, I repeated these warming breaths and stayed as warm as I could while being frozen alive. As soon as I stepped out of the chamber, I could feel it. Warmth, oh, how marvelous was the warmth, like a rush of blood flow. I immediately knew this was a healing experience, triggering *the body* to reduce inflammation and more.

"Nice," I let out, floating up the steps, "Feels like a nice long meditation."

"That would be the rush of endorphins. Your body will continue to reduce inflammation for the next 48 hours. Everything should feel better."

One thing is certain – those are wonderfully positive affirmations, and it is worth it to believe and carry the intention with me. I marveled at the connections with meditation, not only the experience, but the similar purpose of recovery and healing. Cryotherapy is one more thing that is good for meditation, good for *the body,* and good for fitness.

After redressing and floating onto the warm couch in the mobile recovery unit, I remained in a *meditative state,* relaxed, aligned, and focused on aiding the healing process, basking in the aftereffects of the icy cryo glow, my body at peace.

Processes for Reference

9

The Body

———— (————

TODAY IS BEAUTIFUL. The air is light, the temperature perfect. A gentle breeze blows over as a subtle reminder, carrying away worries. The sun rises above the horizon, transitioning into a surreal blend of pinks and oranges glowing from the East. The sky reveals a soft blue backdrop. Wispy, peaceful clouds float high above as a canvas for the luminescent, morphing colors; the water on our right shimmers with the same hues. Monet would appreciate this scenery. When I moved to this humble, blessed lake, I knew this was where I would write.

Ducks and other funny little birds float by and flutter about their business as we place one foot and one paw in front of the other. God and everything good is present here, and it is okay to be happy. Nothing needs to be wrong; everything is okay just the way it is. No matter how perfect the day, sometimes I have to give myself permission and grace to be happy. And no matter how the day appears, it is up to me to find the beauty and perfection in it.

Allie and Stella enjoy these precious moments as well, perhaps their favorite time of day. These meditative walks around the lake help to get my body and energy moving. As an integral part of *the practice,* today is deemed a day of rest, recovery, and healing for *the body.* Dedicating time for taking care of my body is essential to maintaining a consistent practice. Soreness from recent training and stiffness from sleeping lessen with each step. Like the sun coming over the horizon, my body lightens as each foot kisses the earth while the other floats up and forward. Crossing paths, I offer others a smile and a subtle bow of my head. I practice smiling from within, smiling with my eyes, my heart, and my being, exuding love, peace, and joy, believing it is possible to inspire in the simple passing of one another. This reminds me that my life matters, and this is in stark contrast to earlier days, when perhaps inner conflict and misery could be witnessed at a glance instead of peace and happiness. We all have the ability to make the world a better place, and one thing I know to be true, I'm not much good for the world when I'm not happy. But if others can see me soulfully happy, perhaps it will help provide a spark for their ongoing journey.

I look across the lake to see a boot camp in session with fitness mats spread about a well-kept area of grass. Twenty or so participants are doing kettlebell swings and pushups. When the path bends for us to face them directly, they begin to run toward us. Joy lights the way with each step we take, breathing and meditating. The boot campers breeze past us one by one, the air brushing our cheeks. We hear their many unique breaths. Allie and

Stella watch them carefully, and we witness something greater at work. Looking into the runners' eyes, I see beyond any physical limitations to the being inside who is doing the pushing. I see determination through the strain of physical exertion. Their windows to the soul reveal something greater than their physical selves. *The body* has allowed them to awaken this presence and do this work. How magnificent is *the body* to allow us to experience this playground of Earth, our physical existence, *the workout,* and so much more.

Beyond the boot camp, a sacred rock calls my name, where I pause and sit for a brief meditation before turning around. Sitting for even a moment is symbolic and makes a difference. These daily walks have meant a lot to me as a consistent practice, part of my spiritual prescription. Many messages for the book came to life on these treks, and on days when I do nothing else, these walks are *the practice.* For this I thank Allie and Stella, for taking care of them helps me take better care of me.

Upon returning home, I wash my hands at the bathroom sink and stare at my reflection amid the words and images that have collected on the mirror, drawn with window crayons. In the upper-right corner, a heart bursts with beams of purplish reds and blues. Below that, a radiant being meditates in a circle of yellow rays. In between those are words that carry deeper meaning: "KARMA^2, FULL DEVOTION, BE IN THE PRESENCE, HOME, SING YOUR SONG, BELIEVE." Higher intentions have long been underway. On the far left side of the mirror, a column of small starbursts aligns vertically, representing the primary chakras.

Many years ago, this chakra system awakened me to the importance of color, and I now find great joy in something so simple, drawn to a life of balanced and vibrant color. The line of stars ascends in hues from red, orange, and yellow, to green, blue, fuchsia, purple, and white, drawn to correspond with the chakra location in my body when I see my reflection in the mirror. I step to my left until the chakras reflect my own and immediately sense a powerful presence and alignment. My spine straightens without my conscious effort. After a moment, I bring my hands in to face each other and encircle the reflected root chakra. A gentle sensation of energy fills the space between my hands as I hold the red starburst before moving up the system, each chakra with different sensations, clearing, opening, balancing, and aligning. When finished, my hands know what to do and return to my sides. My body begins to blur as I align my vision with the third eye, resting in this Divine upper chakra at the center of my forehead. Just then, my body appears to disappear, as though I can see into the mirror and through myself to the wall behind me. I follow the meditation and recognize my body as pure light and energy – featureless in the outline of space I occupy, as though I am witnessing my spiritual body for the first time. My heart spills laughter upon this connection, overflowing with joy, and when my blissful, watery eyes regain focus, I am beaming as a radiant being.

"Welcome home," whispers the Universe.

I do not see the same person or the same body I once knew. I see the spiritual being I've always known is here. I see the light in my eyes, a kind and happy soul, at peace and one with my body.

Meditative fitness is *the body,* integrating, moving, and healing. In *the practice,* we listen to *the body* and set intentions accordingly. We practice transcending the physical realm. We practice tuning in to *the body* and residing within ourselves. We work on creating a clean and clear body with rising energy. We nurture our relationships with our bodies, change the stories we tell ourselves, and transform the way we see our bodies. *The practice* is an act of love toward your body, and a healthy body helps you reach new levels in meditation and fitness.

"You are not your body," Scott loves to say when you are pushing your limits, overcome with physical sensations. "You are more than your body." The same as we are more than our thoughts, we are more than our physical form. *The workout* gives you the opportunity to rise above the physical, to transcend the pain of physical exertion, to transcend *the body,* which is often capable of more than we think and feel. Meditation gives you a similar opportunity as you learn to sit or stand completely still, which again heightens your *inner senses,* helping you to connect with your energy and transcend identifying yourself only as a body. For your spiritual life, the danger is engaging your practice from a place of vanity, overly concerned about your physical self. This has a downward pull and can cause you to obsess over your body and be overly critical, engaging from a negative place, never being happy with your body because it's never enough. It is a slippery slope and a metaphor for material, surface-level living. The more we obsess and identify ourselves as a body, the lower our vibration and level of consciousness. In the spiritual practice of fitness, we engage from a greater place and for greater reasons than just *the body.*

The body is an expression of heart, mind, and being, reflecting your inner world, values, love, and care. The spiritual body (also known as the celestial, astral, metaphysical, or energy body) is the life and energy in and around the physical form. The physical body is the ultimate instrument, allowing us to infinitely play and create and experience the physical world. *Meditative fitness* as a spiritual practice is the Divine merging and integrating of the physical and spiritual bodies.

Your body makes a difference in the karma of your life. What we do with our bodies and how we treat ourselves determines the lifestyle we lead. The path goes through our humanity. To connect more fully with the Divine, we must connect more fully with that which makes us human. *The body* is part of us in physical existence and represents one of *the four key areas.* The other three represent the metaphysical, and they are all interdependent. A healthy body promotes a healthy spirit, heart, and mind. When we are physically ill, it can be more challenging to find peace, and if we need to raise our physical health, perhaps the best place to start is with mental, emotional, and spiritual health. You often hear this in testimonies of those who have overcome serious injury or life-threatening illness against the odds. It starts with belief and the will to live.

When an imbalance exists in *the body*, there is also an emotional, spiritual, or mental imbalance waiting to be resolved in your practice. Many lessons are found through these challenges. Mental, emotional, and spiritual pains can manifest as a host of physical ailments. The more spiritually integrated you are with your body, the greater your chance of ongoing health, and the greater your abilities in fitness and meditation. Through this integration, we are able to practice a deeper level of healing. We become better athletes and better humans. It is through this union that we realize all that we are here on Earth. We make the most of this physical form and overcome the challenges of our bodies. The goal in spiritual practice is to be one with your body, and when the time comes, to be able to leave your body willingly. Through this peaceful union, rather than holding on in attachment to your body and this life, you learn to let go, for there is always something greater at work.

While genetics play a role, your body is a conscious choice and must be a priority if you want it to be healthy. Through your physical and meditation practices, you flip genetic switches. You change which genes are active. Science and spirituality walk hand-in-hand. You can shape, mold, and create your body in your inner world as well as through your workouts and the foods you eat. More important, however, is your spiritual life. An athletic body will not bring happiness if your inner world is amuck. Happiness comes first; *the practice* is about the journey and experience, not an end physical result. Instead, it is an ever evolving process as we age as gracefully as possible.

The physical is very temporary. You can spend years building strength and conditioning, yet it only takes a short time to lose much of what you have gained. No matter what, we will age, and we don't get to take our bodies with us in the end. In some ways, none of it matters, and in other ways, everything matters. By taking care of your body, by creating a healthy lifestyle, you change the course of your life and beyond.

Transforming your body depends on what you believe about yourself – the way you see yourself and the stories you tell yourself about your body. If you can never see yourself any other way, or if you never acknowledge the truths that reside within you, then you are never going to be any other way. The choice is yours, and the choice is in your actions and the steps you take. Where do you place the importance? Is food or television or something else more important? Are there really any excuses? Or simply priorities? This is a time for honesty and finding motivation from within. Change happens from the inside out. How much do you want to change? Your actions speak louder than anything you tell yourself. Acknowledging your truth is powerful; if you are unhealthy and "out of shape," the truth is that you have chosen to be, whether consciously or not. Argue this and you argue your limitations. Truth that motivates change can often feel harsh. My truth is that I don't want anyone to feel bad about themselves; I only want you to feel good about yourself, to love where you are and who you are right now, but no one else can give that to you. You must find it within yourself.

Many times, we are in denial or delusion about how we arrived where we are, and we don't acknowledge the driving forces under the surface. Through *the practice,* you raise your awareness of what you are creating for yourself, and sometimes these truths can hurt.

Again, what are you willing to admit to yourself?

How do you feel toward your body?

How do you treat your body?

Do you love your body?

Do you care for your body?

How do you think your body feels and responds as a result?

Is there anything more sacred than your sacred space?

What I would like you to hear and let into your heart is that you are beautiful exactly as you are. At the same time, you can have *the body* your heart desires. Just be careful not to seek fulfillment through materialism and vanity, for, again, a seemingly better body does not mean you will find love and happiness; however, if you find love and happiness within you now, your body will respond. If you want to love your body, it starts right now. Forgive yourself for prior self-destructive thoughts and behaviors, for any harm you've done to your body, and start anew. Right here, right now, move forward in treating yourself – your body – with compassion, love, and care. Set intentions, take action, and take care of your body, always behaving as though you love your body, and soon, you will know no different. *The body* responds quickly and very well to intentions and aligned actions. Speak to your body with loving and encouraging words. As you go through your workouts, practice forgiving yourself for any harm you have done to your body, and practice forgiving your body for any troubles it has given you. Forgiveness and gratitude* are close relatives, both with powerful vibrations for more love, peace, and joy. See what happens when you practice them while exerting yourself physically. Think about what your body is allowing you to do. When your legs, arms, hands, and shoulders are burning, tell them how much you love them, forgive yourself for eating poorly or anything else you need to forgive yourself for. "I love you, legs and feet. I love you, knees and elbows. I love you, hands and arms. I love you, heart and lungs. I forgive you for any pain and challenges you've given me, and I forgive myself for not taking better care of you."

After finishing the brief but powerful mirror meditation, I head into the main loft-style living space where a couple of dense foam rollers lean against the wall. Organized on top of Stella's old crate is a purple yoga mat with matching blocks, a massage stick with handles on the ends, a bamboo scraper, some floss bands, a green stretch strap, a five-inch massage ball, two softer ones for the stomach, and a couple of smaller lacrosse balls. These tools have been collected over the years for the purpose of myofascial release and physical therapy, instrumental in preventing injury, healing aches and pains, recovering from soreness and stiffness, and promoting the flow of energy. I know that if I neglect this mobility work, I put myself at higher risk of injury. *The body* begs to be moved and mobilized, otherwise it tightens up and problems emerge. Stand, stretch and relax, tighten then loosen, swing, kick, roll, massage, sink into trigger points, open the joints, increase ranges of motion, and live pain free. I grab the foam roller that has knobs all over it and hear a thud as it lands on the carpet.

The knobs press into the soft tissues of my back as I roll along my spine. Looking up at the ceiling, I hear the soft crackling of the roller against the carpet. I feel my nervous system light up, an activation of cells and spark of signals. All that is good for *the body* – all that promotes health, fitness, and the movement of cells and energy, and all that helps one to relax – is good for meditation. Rolling for even a minute or two along the spine helps activate your greatest ally in meditation and fitness: your central nervous system. This is beneficial for the same reason we sit or stand with a straight, vertical spine in meditation. It aids connectivity and the river of energy and signals. The spine is the inner highway and serves as an antenna for Divine transmissions. In *the workout*, you activate, fire, and tax your nervous system. As a perfect complement, in meditation, you learn how to relax and energize your nervous system. From this flow of energy around your spine, you can access your entire body and send conscious signals where needed. From here, you can clear your energy. The primary energy centers run along the spine, and a straight spine aligns with physical, spiritual, and emotional strength. People who are happy and alive tend to walk more upright with their heads held high. If you want to raise your state, you can start by embodying the posture. Meditation and nearly all sports and fitness – *lifts, movements,* and *skills* – are optimally executed with a naturally straight spine.

Massage and foam rolling help prepare you for meditation. I encourage you to test this and feel the difference in your energy. You may notice that your body conducts as a clearer channel. This is similar to the effects of chanting, yoga, and *the workout*, activating cells in *the body* and creating a noticeable vibration. Some of the best times to meditate are after *the workout*, physical yoga, a massage, or foam rolling. These methods help you to relax and "get there" more quickly. A relaxed body aids a relaxed mind and vice-versa. You can sit and relax and give yourself a massage from the inside, a vibration where your entire body feels as though you have just had a physical massage. You can *go in* and create a lightness of being. You can quiet your mind. Although it may take practice and patience, you are capable of doing all of these things through meditation alone. In the beginning, you may have to sit for 10 to 15 minutes before settling into deeper consciousness and a quiet mind. Or, with practice, you can chant for a couple of minutes and find yourself in a *meditative state*. You can foam roll or go through a workout or yoga practice and find a more quiet mind with ease. Examples such as these serve as primers for deeper meditation.

Listening to my body, I roll from my back to my hips and legs, pausing at tight tender spots, pondering my level of hydration, food intake, and recent workouts. Similar to meditative stretching* – breathing and relaxing into the stretch – I relax and breathe into the tightness until I feel a dispersion. My body guides me and lets me know where to focus here the same way it does in warming up for *the workout*. With this communication, you can release tension where needed and increase your ranges of motion; you can improve the karma of your body and prevent injuries.

Determining what is truly healthy or "good for you" can be challenging. You can easily find contradictory studies, and it can be hard to know what to trust, but what you can learn to rely on is your inner knowing. Your body provides constant feedback, and no one knows your body as well as you. No one else lives in your body. No one else can change your body and your health as much as you can. Prior to eating or drinking, ask your inner wisdom whether something is good for you and pay close attention to your intuition. In making any decision, ask whether it promotes strength. You will know the answer based on your inner response. While we may not always be right, it is about developing the intuition and wise discernment.

By raising your awareness, listening to your body, and paying attention to the way you respond to stimuli, you continue to learn what is good for you and what promotes strength. Your inner wisdom also knows when to rest and when to engage in *the workout*, knows what areas of *the body* to prepare and where to focus mobility efforts. *The body* too has its consciousness; it knows when something is good for it or not and reacts accordingly with either a strong or weak response. In weak responses, *the body* triggers healing. When there is a high degree of this happening, it constantly requires extra energy and blood flow and can culminate in chronic fatigue. Regular exposure to anything that is not good for us can be life-draining and spirit-shrinking, leading to numerous physical and mental *abnormalities*. *The practice* is to connect with the consciousness of your body and nervous system, to align so that everything within you is functioning in harmony. *The practice* is to aid the otherwise automatic functions of *the body*, and to promote a strong response.

Regardless of how your body feels, know that there is a reason it feels the way it does. If you wake up stiff, heavy, and foggy, know there is a reason for it, and it is not the norm. It is not your curse. Rather than being excuses to refrain from your practice, they become part of it. We choose to love and respect ourselves and not accept a low state of being. We don't settle for not feeling well. Instead, we answer *the call* and rise in determination to new heights of wellness.

A simple measure and basic rule to bring into awareness: the more stiff and achy your joints, tight your muscles, or tired your mind, the less clean and clear your body is. Above the normal aspects of recovery from your training, recognize these signals to mean that your body is in a state of reaction, rejection, or resistance. When we are clear, meditation and *the workout* reflect this clarity with strength and energy flowing freely. In addition to benefits in spiritual practice, you are more likely to reach your fitness goals with a clean and clear physical body – goals such as weight loss or increased strength, conditioning, and work capacity. Whatever they are for you, may they all be for the purpose of something greater, for what they mean to you at a deeper level.

The body is constantly changing and healing with new cells replacing old. *The workout* equals change and awakening at the cellular level, where cells are active and alive with a higher rate of turnover. Muscle tissue repairs. *The body* heals, recovers, and adapts. Even injuries can serve to make us better by exposing weaknesses. Growth and healing often come with some degree of pain or discomfort. Whether stepping out of your comfort zone, acknowledging the depths of your heart, overcoming injuries, or encountering soreness from yesterday's workout, being free of pain may require moving through the pain.

Rolling back and forth on the foam roller guides me toward my meditation cushion. It simply makes sense to take advantage of a relaxed body with activated cells. A tight body is closed while a relaxed body is open, ready to receive with free-flowing energy. Tension can reside in your heart, your mind, or your body. Just like rolling on the foam roller releases physical tension, in meditation, we release it all. We release any inner pressure that has been building. We open our hearts and release tension in our minds that has a tendency to create stress and erratic behavior. And all of this can start by relaxing your body. As a regular practice, pay particular attention to your hands, face, feet, and shoulders, and release tension whenever it comes into your awareness.

In *the workout*, we "get tight" to lift a heavy weight or execute a certain movement pattern. We contract the appropriate muscles, but this does not mean we want to tighten up overall. Instead, we contract when we need to and stay relaxed overall. Being able to relax at will can help you recover more quickly while in the middle of intense exertion, which includes relaxing your heart rate and breathing. Maintaining a lower heart rate in a tough workout allows you to complete more work over time. Staying relaxed helps you conserve energy while tightening up results in undue fatigue and lower performance. When a swimmer tightens at the end of a race, he or she slows down and loses the race. In golf, tennis, and other sports, when you tighten up, you are more prone to miss the shot or make a mistake. Tension arrests the flow of energy and results in slower movement. For example, with a tight grip on a golf club, tennis racquet, or even a jump rope, you lose swing speed. If your entire body is tight, your movement is slow and heavy. If you stay loose, however, you are able to move with quick, explosive contractions, speed, grace, and momentum. Your movement is more athletic. Imagine a tall box jump where you explode from the ground yet stay relaxed and fluid in the air; you use the momentum as it carries you, pulling your legs up in perfect timing as gracefully as you can. With less resistance, fluid movement equals flowing energy and takes your performance to higher levels.

I crawl a few feet from the roller to my beloved cushion. Like a breath of fresh air, special energy is found in this space. I sit in half lotus and lengthen my spine. I rotate, stretch, and open my hips, legs, knees, and ankles. I get comfortable and balanced, settling into a position I can sit in for a period of time. Immediately, my spine connects and locks in as universal antenna, automatically rising and straightening, a sense worth remembering and repeating. I sit perfectly vertical with a natural arch, centered on the edge of the cushion with my legs complementing each other like two puzzle pieces. The first breath after closing my eyes is programmed to ground and settle into a *meditative state.* I go there with a long, slow exhale, surveying the space in and around my body, sensing and envisioning the spiritual body as it appeared in the mirror. This is where I live, in this space of this body.

Tuning in and familiarizing yourself with this space allows you to do inner work in relation to your body, helps you nurture your body and let go of addictive, mental friction you may carry. By tuning in to *the body,** you increase your sensitivity for the purpose of unlocking hidden abilities. Once practiced, you can quickly use your breath to scan up and down your body to determine whether you are centered and aligned. If you feel an area out of alignment, you can make a correction. This may feel like something is out of place, or like the energy is not traveling in a straight line. You may feel out of balance or off-center even though you are sitting perfectly straight. This reflects your inner balance and centeredness. You will notice the flow of energy change as you breathe up and down your body and as you set the intention to center and align, from the base of your spine to the top of your head and beyond. For an added uplifting practice, rotate or spin your energy upward around your spine with your breath.

In fitness and sports, it is beneficial to imagine your movement emanating from the center of your spine. Again, your body provides constant feedback in your *lifts* and *movements*. This is an aspect of intuitive athleticism to be developed and enhanced, the ability to feel movement, to feel a particular *lift* or *skill*, to feel when the most efficient muscles are recruited. When it happens, it feels fluid and right, and the weight feels lighter. This is not a thinking process, but a feeling process. *Meditative fitness* helps develop this sensory feedback.

Still tuning in, I sense a subtle vibration in and around the back of my neck. I go into the vibration with the intention of expanding, not through control but rather by allowing and magnifying the energy and sensation. The vibration expands to my head. A tingling sensation on top of my head indicates my crown chakra is opening. Like a higher presence awakening, chills stream down my body. The vibration expands to my throat, across my shoulders, and down my spine, which lengthens with each rising inhale. The vibration lifts the entire space of my upper body. A vibration like this allows us to send signals throughout the central nervous system, tapping into *pure intention* with ease. A vibration like this allows us to practice healing. This is the vibration that feels like an inner massage at the cellular level. The possibilities are infinite. This vibration feels as peaceful, loving, and as good as anything I have ever felt. This vibration feels like God.

I move with the vibration from my spine to my arms and hands, which immediately rise a couple of inches above my knees, suspended in the air, and not through physical effort. I have practiced this before, but never have they risen so quickly or effortlessly. My arms, along with my entire upper body, are lifted and held up by the vibration. I am not physically holding my posture anymore. It is simply there, floating in place, and everything is right. I feel as if I could float up in the air at any moment, as though I can sustain this levitation for as long as I allow.

This is about moving toward the light. Close your eyes, take a deep breath, and take a moment to imagine what life is like without a body. Imagine it in all of your magnificence, a pure being with intention, presence, and awareness. Now, imagine having that with you and think about everything your body allows you to do and experience, living this life. Find a place of love and gratitude toward your body.

My love and gratitude is plentiful in these precious moments. I release my arms to return at rest on top of my legs. I open my eyes and ensure I am fully here, fully present, reorienting from a deeper state. My body and soul are at peace – clear, light, and relaxed. Having not yet eaten today, it is time to give my body some food.

Processes for Reference

Food

BLESSINGS WERE UNFOLDING, but at the time I was 22 years old, and something was seriously wrong with me. My physical life had gone from highly active to mostly sedentary. My food intake, however, remained high. I often prided myself on eating more than people twice my size, and I never worried about the foods I ate. Among my greatest eating triumphs, I remember eating an entire box of macaroni and cheese followed by a large pepperoni pizza. Consuming two double-meat footlong sandwiches in one sitting was common, and I once ate nine TV dinners back-to-back just to see how many I could eat. I often ate a whole day's worth of calories in single meals. People always asked me where I put it and told me I was lucky. What they didn't know was that after eating, I more often than not experienced shortness of breath, heart palpitations, painful bloating, knots in my stomach, and irritable bowels. Chronic fatigue had set in to the point where I regularly passed out at 9pm, unable to keep my eyes open. I fell sick multiple times a year with a cold, sinus infection, or bronchitis with coughing that lasted for months at a time. Intuition told me something had to be seriously wrong. I thought perhaps I was developing diabetes or some other life-threatening condition. As time passed, the symptoms appeared to be chronic, and despite intuition, I believed this was all somehow "normal."

While my eating was perhaps at an all-time low, after my tennis career, I dedicated myself to passing the PGA playing ability test, which is required to become a certified golf professional. While preparing for this mentally and physically grueling challenge, on my first and last swing of a practice round, I felt a sharp pop in my back upon extending in the follow through. Each breath thereafter was painful and forcibly shallow. Upon seeking medical attention, I discovered that I had unhooked a rib from my spine. Not only that, but I also had other spine issues as a sign of further deterioration of my body.

"How could this be happening? I'm only 22 and my body is falling apart." With a flair for the inner dramatic, I really thought I was somehow dying. Life was draining out of me. It seemed impossible to be happy or have any sense of well-being, which was also part of my "normal." Meanwhile, nothing showed up on medical tests, and on the outside, I appeared lean and healthy. Chiropractic care helped for 30 minutes at a time before my back tightened again. Pain and discomfort were my constant companions with no solution in sight. Still, I continued with determination, well-practiced at coping and living this way, and I managed to pass the playing ability test.

Soon thereafter, hope arrived through my first big spiritual awakening. Like a flash of lightning, everything, including my entire life, made sense. It was like seeing and hearing the truth for the first time. From this moment on, I allowed this light to guide me. I pursued and devoted myself to spiritual growth, knowing it was the only way for me to truly live and have any chance at happiness and well-being. With newfound hope and a positive new environment, I stumbled upon a chiropractor/nutritionist who forever changed my life and sent me on a lifelong journey of digestive health. Through a process of kinesiology muscle testing, which can determine the foods or stimuli that produce a strong or weak response for your body, I learned I was reactive to wheat/gluten, dairy, and chocolate. Due to the high frequency of the former two in my diet, my body was malnourished and breaking down.

The world of food as I knew it came crashing down on me. "No more pizza?! This cannot be true," I rejected, feeling the need to prove it for myself. It was the only way for me to believe, the same as renouncing faith and belief in order to truly find them.

Through my own observations in treating my life as an ongoing experiment, sure enough, all the symptoms and *abnormalities* were amplified upon ingesting wheat and dairy, even when I wasn't aware I had eaten them until after the fact.

In the process of coming to terms with my new reality, I began to learn about digestive health. In combination with personal experience over many years, I grew to know some basic universal truths related to food. And if this is not a complete list, feel free to add to it for yourself and your own well-being.

1. **Digestive health is directly related to all health.**
   No matter what is happening in your overall health, it is linked to your digestive health. Food is not the only

factor or variable, but it can be the root factor, and it makes the difference for better or worse. If you fall sick or are not feeling well in any way, ask yourself: "What foods have I been eating?" and "Is this related to the way I've been eating?"

2. **There are foods that are easy to break down and easy on the digestive system, and there are foods that are hard to break down and hard on the digestive tract.** The goal with digestion is to break down and absorb our food and nutrients while efficiently eliminating waste. Foods that leave your body the same way they entered can be more taxing on your digestive tract, which is especially important when there is already damage or if you are in a highly reactive state.

3. **Many of us unknowingly ingest foods that we are sensitive or reactive to.** These foods produce a weak response, and your body rejects them. In many cases, they are overly prevalent foods in your diet, overloading your system until it develops a response. Treated as a foreign substance by *the body,* these foods can trigger an immune response and weaken the immune system, contributing to illness, inflammation, and ailments. In addition, they can also dull our spirits and drain our energy.

4. **At any point in time, we can carry around 5-10 unnecessary pounds of inflammation in our gut and body.** This can feel like a constant bloating in your stomach accompanied by heavy energy and blood flow. A painful or raw feeling on an empty stomach can be a sign of

inflammation and a lingering reaction in your gut, often felt most prevalently in the morning. When you clear up the foods causing the damage and heal your digestive system, bloating recedes, and you no longer feel pain when hungry.

5. **Joint pain and other forms of pain involve inflammation.** While inflammation can sometimes be healthy for healing, an inflamed digestive system contributes to over-inflamed joints, muscles, connective tissue, lungs, and overall body. Wherever there is pain, inflammation is likely present. With the foods we eat and a healthy digestive system, we can greatly reduce inflammation, accelerate healing, and in turn, reduce pain and symptoms. Some common inflammation culprits include sugar, artificial sweeteners, wheat/gluten, dairy, soy, corn, fried foods, rancid oil, and highly acidic, processed, or high-sodium foods.

6. **Processed, genetically modified, or artificial foods tend to produce a weak response.** Manufactured foods can be harder to break down, and they can contribute to a build-up of toxicity in your body. It is no surprise that a factory-produced pastry, with a long list of unpronounceable chemical ingredients, does not promote strength.

7. **Natural, whole, organic, "real" foods promote a strong response.** These are foods with a single ingredient or a small number of recognizable ingredients. They promote a strong response unless one is sensitive and reactive to the specific food. Rarely, however, are we reactive to organic meats, vegetables, and rice.

8. **It is best to maintain consistent blood-sugar levels.**
Big swings in blood-sugar levels lead to mood swings.
Spikes and crashes contribute to instability. Low blood
sugar can contribute to a low state of being. These levels
are impacted directly by sugar and also our balance of
foods. High sugar consumption can trigger inflammation
and contribute to illness and other ailments. Inconsistent
blood-sugar levels also play a role in metabolic issues, fat
storage, and decreased muscle production.

9. **A balance of lean protein, healthy fat, and complex carbohydrates promotes healthy functioning.**
While each of us may have different needs, all of these
macronutrients are important for fuel, recovery, and
strength. Protein is the number one building block for
your body and muscles. Healthy fats provide further
fuel for our brains and metabolism. Vegetables and
complex carbs provide important fiber and micronutrients. Fats and low glycemic carbs help slow digestion
and provide sustaining fuel, which can help balance
blood sugar levels and aid recovery from workouts.
Healthy fats also help *the body* let go of fat rather than
hold on out of need.

10. **Water, water, and more water.** Hydration is essential for
digestive and overall health. Your body and organs function better in every way when hydrated. Water supports
the body's natural cleansing process. It is a conductor
of energy in *the body,* and it aids blood flow and oxygen delivery. Hydration helps prevent pockets of energy

from becoming trapped, such as knots or tight muscles. Whether it is a training day or rest day, muscles will be more or less tense or relaxed depending on our levels of hydration and the foods we consume. More than water, hydration includes electrolytes such as salt and potassium, which are important when we are losing or consuming high quantities of water. Muscle cramps, headaches, and fatigue from dehydration are commonly related to salt and potassium levels, and when we drink an abundance of water, we run the risk of diluting these levels as well. When referring to food in this chapter, we are also referring to hydration.

After I made peace with giving up pizza and nearly all the rest of my everyday foods, I embarked on a 21-day metabolic (digestive) cleansing process: a three-day liquid fast with hypoallergenic, medical-grade protein shakes, followed by 18 days of three shakes a day plus one balanced, hypoallergenic meal. By the second day of the liquid fast, the symptoms began to disappear. My breathing improved. The lingering cough subsided. My feet, knees, and spine stopped aching. Within one week, I lost nine pounds of inflammation, more than six percent of my body weight. All swelling and painful bloating was gone. I looked and felt amazing. Radiant. Strong. Clear. My mind, sharp. The tension in my back and other muscles disappeared. I was able to hold a chiropractic adjustment for the first time. My energy soared as I stayed awake past 9pm. All symptoms and *abnormalities* went away. I felt like I could walk on air, better than I had ever felt. I came to the realization that I had likely been suffering from negative reactions to food my entire life.

"This is normal?! If this is normal, then this is crazy!" I experienced a sense of well-being for the first time. Although foreign, this was *the new normal,* and I never could have imagined how good normal feels.

Meditative fitness is food for lightness of being and lightness afoot, food for strength, energy, higher consciousness, and greater physical and metaphysical abilities. Foods in alignment with *the practice* help you create a clear body at the cellular level. The way you eat becomes part of your spiritual practice as you develop your lifestyle, find your *new normal,* and improve your relationship with food.

We can give away our power to anything we choose, food being a big one. We can be a slave to hunger and blind to what we are putting in our bodies. Or we can rise to new levels and allow food to serve a higher purpose, higher intention, and have new meaning.

Food has similar effects on *the workout,* meditation, and your flow of energy. It can either be a natural cure, miracle medicine, or a poison running through you. Food is energy and fuel for the ultimate instrument of *the body.* It is part of the foundation of your lifestyle. What you consume makes the difference in reaching your fitness and body related goals. If you want to change the chemistry of your body, you do so with *the workout* and food. Commonly known in the fitness world, you can train and train and not see results until key nutritional elements are addressed. The same can prove true for your happiness and spiritual life.

Food plays a big role in your karma with all the related causes and effects. Food consumption and digestion help determine your metabolism (how efficiently you burn fuel), which impacts your accessible energy and whether you feel heavy and slow or light, energized, and alive.

A heavy stomach equals a heavy body with lethargic energy. Eat poorly and *the workout* suffers. Eat poorly, and meditation, *the breath*, and energy suffer. When we eat poorly, we are less likely to feel like meditating or exercising in the first place. We are less likely to want to get out of bed in the morning – the dreaded food hangover. On the other end of the spectrum, eat well and wake up with an abundance of energy. Breathe deeply and clearly. Experience a relaxed body at peace. Eat well, and love *the body* you are in. Enhance your workouts, meditations, and life.

The workout goes hand in hand with this building block of food, aiding digestive health and metabolism. Exercise helps burn and convert food to fuel. With a faster turnover of cells, there is less reactivity and developed sensitivities to food. *The workout* also promotes eating clean, for eating poorly increases the "pain" felt in rigorous exertion. You can feel toxicity pulse through your body in a workout the same way you can feel it with heightened senses in meditation. This can be felt at the cellular level like a subtle throbbing with each heartbeat. In addition, tight muscles and inflamed joints due to a poor diet increase your risk of injury. Allow your practice to help you make better decisions by consuming foods in alignment with your well-being and the demands being placed on your body. Eating enough food and a balance of quality foods are both essential to recovery after strenuous exercise. Our degree of soreness can depend on how well we eat and hydrate. If we recover poorly, we may feel less strong in our next workout. When we pick up a barbell or move our body, food makes a difference as to whether we feel strong or weak in the exertion. It can either help us to be lighter on our feet or it can cause us to be more sluggish. Chances are that many of you have lived that experiment in your workouts. If you want to make the most of your time spent in *the workout*, you need proper nutrition. There is no way to truly offer your best without the best support of food.

Every day we are faced with the choice of what to eat. We make decisions, set intentions, and strengthen our will to sustain them. We all have our patterns and habits with food, and each of us can develop our personal guidelines that culminate in our way of life, which can evolve and change alongside the needs and chemistry of our bodies and the options provided by the world around us. Take great care in sorting through all that is available in the marketplace, and seek counsel from trusted sources. In this way, we all do the best we can with our current food karma.

You choose the ingredients of your life. You can serve yourself whatever you want based on available resources and your ability, and you can learn and rise in the process. When stocking your home restaurant, where you are the executive chef, purchase foods that you know are good for you and align with strength. Not only does this have the potential to save you money, but also temptation and grief. It simply doesn't make sense to pay money to feel bad. Invest in foods that help you feel good, and may you get to the point where feeling good tastes better than any foods you crave.

Remember, the game is simple.

How good can you feel?

How healthy and clear can you be?

Normal is unique to you and what you know to be familiar. Normal for a lot of us has been living with any number of *abnormalities* such as low, tired energy, frequent illness, indigestion, joint pain, or headaches. This does not have to be "normal." Sick and tired doesn't have to be a way of life. There is a chance that much of what you have experienced thus far is not "normal," but rather a constant state of reaction and inflammation. We work on and clear *abnormalities* in *the practice*. As another form of *the challenge*, they call us to rise to the opportunity and test our ability to heal. Other *abnormalities* could be any of the following: emotional instability and moodiness, chronic knots and tight muscles, inflamed fascia, tendonitis, shortness of breath, painful bloating and other stomach pains, excessive gas, inflamed bowels, back pain, and other body aches. *Abnormalities,* like our overall health, are connected to the foods we eat and our digestive health.

When we are clean and clear, illness and injury aren't vibrational matches. To step into change, we step into the unknown and let go of the old familiar. *The new normal* is feeling magnificent, awake with an abundance of energy, a sense of well-being, *the body* at peace. *The new normal* is when your body is in harmony with everything you put into it, digesting with ease and smooth, consistent bowel movements. *The new normal* is a sharp mind, clear body, and light spirit. When we get a taste of what "normal" is really like, it is astounding how good it feels, and there is no turning back.

The healthier you become, the more aware of your state of being you become. The more pure your system, the more aware you are of your reactions to foods. How frequently you react to foods and the amount of *abnormalities* experienced are measures of your digestive health. Chronic *abnormalities* are a sign of regular consumption of sensitive or intolerant foods. If you identify and eliminate foods you are sensitive to, yet you still experience reactions, then you may have damage in your gut that needs some time to heal. When in this highly reactive state, we have a tendency to be less stable. We are more likely to be irritable, anxious, depressed, or lack an overall sense of well-being. Know that all of this can heal over time with food as part of your practice.

To help realize your *new normal,* raise your awareness of what you put in your body and how you feel as a result. Food carries intention, and our consumption provides continuous feedback. The more tuned in you are to your body and energy, the more you will know which foods are good for you. You can tell if you are operating at optimum energy and if you are digesting well. You can sense when you have low blood-sugar. Pay attention. Learn the combinations of foods that work and don't work well for you. This is an evolving process of navigating and nurturing your relationship with food. Take notice of *abnormalities.* Trends will emerge to help you determine which foods to eliminate and which foods to navigate toward. Whenever you feel tired, trust your inner wisdom to know whether the tired energy is related to your gut. To heighten this sense, close your eyes, and with a deep breath, survey the energy locationally in your body. As you gather and release energy with your breath, see if you can sense a connection among the locations where the energy is found. Gather, release, and exchange for clear and awake energy until you feel a shift. Clearing tired energy may come with some physiological phenomena, and it may require going through an even heavier tired feeling before making it to the other side. In any process, it is important to run it through to completion.

For higher levels of fitness, clarity, and consciousness, and to prevent having to clear undesired energy daily, consume foods free of anything that clouds your energy. In the process of eating clean, you align with strength and transform yourself into an efficient fuel-burning machine. Not only does it help your performance in *the workout* and reduce the sensations at a high intensity, but it also promotes being a clear channel in meditation, better able to perceive Divine wisdom, guidance, and vision.

Determining what to eat in those early new-way-of-life days proved challenging. Nearly everything I normally ate was off the menu, and finding gluten-free food those many years ago proved difficult as well. I waited patiently for the world around me to catch on to what was happening to us in relation to food. I knew it was only a matter of time before things would change, and now, there are more gluten-free options and healthy places to eat than ever before. I still get excited each time I find a new healthy option at a mainstream grocery or restaurant. As our consciousness is rising, we are migrating toward more pure versions of foods. We have become more aware of how we respond to food in this modern era.

My initial food awakening led to a long-term process of growth in my relationship with food. I had to let go of all the foods I so dearly cherished and the accompanying feelings of lack. I had days when nothing sounded good to eat. I had days when the only foods that sounded good were the foods that were killing me, days where I really didn't feel like eating, where it felt like a hassle I could easily do without. I felt better not eating than I did eating many foods. Not only were these days an emotional response to food as a mood enhancer, but I also had a low appreciation for food.

As I grew, I started taking care of myself. I developed a passion for healthy gourmet cooking, creating and combining recipes, trying new things, and substituting ingredients where needed. Advanced planning became important, regular trips to the grocery, preparing multiple meals at a time, and making sure I knew what I would eat the next day. Cooking for myself began to feel like really living, and healthy cooking became a form of love and care.

The years were filled with periods of doing better or worse, managing detours, testing limits, treating myself to pizza and accepting the consequences. I was cleared on dairy a couple of years after the initial testing, a sign of better digestive health, and it became common to live gluten-free six days a week with one treat day, followed by mild reactions.

I was able to continue on that way for quite a while until, while writing this book, I had a relapse of sorts. Within the time span of a couple of months, my knee developed lingering pain and swelling. I had a flare-up of pharyngitis and then bronchitis, both exactly two days after eating pizza. All too familiar, the lingering cough was back. Next came the worst allergies and asthma I have ever experienced. Yes, it was allergy season, but it was more than that. My joints spontaneously experienced some degree of pain, similar to arthritis. A wrist, an elbow, shoulder, knee, neck, or back. The surrounding muscles and fascia were tight and inflamed like a bundle of nerves and knots. This too was becoming normal again. All of these would pop up and linger before going away as quickly as they arrived after a couple of consecutive days of eating clean. Pain can spontaneously appear and disappear, which is a good reason to believe in our miraculous ability to heal. To top it off, as a perfect example of karma, while coughing my way through a workout, I pulled a small muscle near the same spot I popped a rib out those many years ago. Once again, I had to come to terms with the truth – my entire body, including my lungs, throat, joints, and most of all, my gut, was inflamed. I felt like a big walking ball of inflammation. I was reacting to dairy again, and I could no longer get away with my detours. Rock bottom happened in the middle of the night. After eating garlic bread at dinner, I woke up coughing so hard I was nearly choking and puking all at once, gasping for air. I couldn't go on like that anymore. I knew I had to do something. It was time to recommit to my health.

I started immediately. The parameters were set: consume only real food, free of gluten, dairy, added sugar, and artificial sweeteners. I planned for a metabolic detox similar to the one 12 years prior, which included a nutritionally rich liquid fast to help reset the digestive system.

A modified fast can help eliminate inflammation and *abnormalities* related to digestive health, which is like returning your system to the purity of a newborn. In addition to health reasons, a fast can symbolize devotion and discipline as you transcend the primal urges of hunger and cravings. Refraining from habits and behaviors can be spiritually cleansing and unlock flows of energy. The fast, however long, can serve as a conduit for transformation. A new way of life can be much easier to follow after a successful fast. Going without solid food for even a day can strengthen your willpower, shift your perspective, and help heal your relationship with food.

It is easy for us to take our food for granted and not fully appreciate it, especially in its most natural state. In today's world, we are less concerned with how to find and grow our food than we are with the many choices and robust flavors available. We lose sense of what the actual food tastes like, and it doesn't taste good to us plain, in all of its natural glory. Through a fast, you may quickly find gratitude for food in its natural state – even a single piece of broccoli can be the greatest thing in the world.

Like déjà vu, two days into the liquid fast, my allergies, asthma, bronchitis, and cough disappeared, along with any other miscellaneous joint and stomach pains. Within a week I lost 10 pounds of inflammation. The energy previously spent on pain and discomfort was soaring and free. I experienced heightened clarity and lightness of being. My body was at peace again experiencing the magnificent new normal.

Rather than a short-term diet, all of this is about developing a sustainable way of life, related to your truth. We all have a diet, and it is not about short-term or whether you are on or off, have to do this, or have to do that. You can do whatever you want, but there is always karma and consequences to live with.

For a quick meditative process, close your eyes, take a deep breath, and connect with your higher self. Take as much time as you need on each question, reading it and then closing your eyes to find your answer within. First, give yourself permission to eat whatever you want. Make this real to you. You don't have to eat anything or not eat anything. You can eat whatever you want. Take a deep sigh of relief. Next, ask yourself how you would like to feel in your life. What do you want to feel like physically, mentally, emotionally, and spiritually? What does your heart and soul desire? What do you want in your fitness practice? What do you want for your body? See if you can get a taste of that. What does it feel like? What do you see yourself doing? If you need to, simply imagine what it feels like. Give yourself a moment, and when you have it, connected with your heart and soul, ask yourself what you really want to put in your body. For now, you don't need specifics, but how would you like to feel after eating? How would you like to feel in relation to food? What kind of foods do you want to build your home? How do you really want to eat? This is a process of heart and soul level honesty, permission and surrender, where we remove inner resistance, denial, and deprivation on the road to love and gratitude.

This is about deeper motivations in your engagement with food. A process like this can be applied to other subjects and repeated to help you align with your highest good.

This is your life and your way of life, and it is more important than any short-term diet. It isn't all or nothing, black and white. There is no on or off-ramp to your way of life, so even on a detour, you do not quit or give up on it, but simply choose when to return to your most happy and fulfilling way of life. No need for further backsliding, because through *meditative fitness,* you are committed to health. You are committed to food that promotes clear energy and a lightness of being, food that aligns with your workouts, meditations, and vision for your life.

Vision

I FELT SO small as I looked around in awe at all of the larger athletes and the playground of racks and rigs, colorful plates, and loaded barbells. I was mesmerized by the facility and inspired by the rare opportunity. With athletes in preparation and a crowd of onlookers, I breathed in the energy of the place and couldn't help but be more awake and charged.

Earlier in the day, I saw a post online for a local charity competition called "Night of Champions." I texted J.D. to inquire about getting on a team, and eight hours later, I walked through the doors of CrossFit Dallas Central, a renowned affiliate in the community.

After seeing *the workout* online, I had been visualizing the progression all day: from the running, to the clean and jerk, to the burpee box jumps. I would have had to try pretty hard not to think about and visualize what was to come. I wanted to do well. My heart was engaged from the moment I decided to go and compete. Everything that comes up is part of *the practice*, and it was my choice to make sure the visions were of success and triumph over adversity.

Watching the other athletes go through their heats, I was further inspired as men and women hoisted the prescribed weights above their heads with ease. Meanwhile, their teammates performed burpee box jumps at a furious pace. The vision of *the workout* was alive for all to see. In the second heat, J.D. completed one clean and jerk after another, providing me with a perfect vision of the *lift*. I paid close attention to his form and the deliberate breath before the jerk. This was at minimum a two-breath *lift*, one for the clean, and one for the jerk. There is both benefit and difficulty in watching others go first. While gaining insight for *the workout*, you also witness the degree of challenge being confronted, which can be a little nerve-racking. This was no easy endeavor; however, it's all in the way we see things, isn't it? There was so much joy everywhere, underneath any jitters or physical "pain," so much joy and excitement, intense focus and effort, a sense of accomplishment, of significant feats, and the culmination of hard work. This is why people love the sport of fitness.

During the opening 800-meter run of my heat, I upheld my vision for the work to follow. Glancing to my left, I saw my reflection floating along in the storefront windows outside. For the clean and jerk, in the split second before the *lift*, I envisioned the barbell taking off from the ground, traveling as close to my body as possible before landing on my shoulders and being hurled overhead. Each repetition provided vital feedback that I applied to the vision and performance of the next one.

In the burpee box jumps, I saw myself through the eyes of onlookers. As if in one fluid motion, I dove to the deck, caught myself with my hands and feet, sprawled with my chest to the ground before my feet were back under me, launching me up and to the right, landing lightly on the corner of the box, fully extended, then fading back down toward the earth again. From their perspective, I saw the fluidity of movement and the angles of my body. Watching athletes can be as poetic as watching dancers. Movement in fitness isn't so different than dancing – the lines, the form, the technique, leaping into the air, controlling *the body* with precision, back and forth lunges like a salsa, with barbells and boxes serving as stage props. And for each workout, you must the know the choreography.

We were still in the race when fate had it in store for me to take the home stretch of the team carry relay. This was a daunting proposition after already carrying the first leg, not to mention the prior 15 minutes of work, but I had a clear vision of the opportunity, and it couldn't have been more perfect. Erinn jumped up. I caught her legs in good old fashion piggy-back style, not only a much better position than the first leg, but my energy had come back like a high-powered rechargeable battery. I sprinted off like a possessed man and entered a different realm, a guttural place I had perhaps never been before. It was time to see what I was made of, to see how big I was on the inside. It's funny to look back and hear myself.

"Follow me guys! We're going all the way home!" I commanded passionately with a childlike innocence to encourage our larger teammates, carrying only themselves, to try to keep up.

"I...am...not...stopping!" I grunted to Erinn from somewhere deep within, with as much determination as I had ever spoken; the same determination that helped me overcome my challenges in life and find the light. I had to convince my smaller self of that – I won't give up, I won't stop, I won't quit, I will continue, I will live. Otherwise, there was no way I was going to make it.

"Don't worry, I won't drop you." I said to Erinn with all my heart, moving fast with my muscles nearing failure.

"I know you won't," she said. She had confidence in me too, which was all I needed to further fuel me. I had so much love for her and our fellow athletes for sharing in those rare unguarded moments, exposing ourselves raw.

As we approached the corner leading inside the box, a vision struck me, a flash of what was happening. I saw something greater in myself, and it was my turn to inspire. I could hear cheering from inside. They saw me leave with her, and they would see me return with her. I never saw myself exactly like that before, and we often don't realize the difference we make. All of us have the ability to inspire others with what we do, how we live, and how we overcome. Here I was, one of the smaller male competitors of the night, providing a sight to see. When our larger teammates were too spent after the clean and jerks, I practically dragged Erinn out, bent over, with her arms clasped around my neck and her feet barely hovering above the ground.

I was past the point of having anything left when we rounded the final corner. I relied purely on heart and the will to keep going. With each breath and heavy step came primal grunts, like pleading for more strength as my feet dragged across the rocky asphalt. Once inside, I slowed down and calmed the grunting only to hear the roar of the crowd. I made it to the far wall finish line and gently set Erinn on her feet before collapsing on my back, my arms spread out wide, looking up at the ceiling with my chest rising up and down and my heart pounding faster than I had ever felt it.

Tunnel vision had set in back there, in a different world where the effort was all there was. I later had the thought that other teams may have already finished; however, in those moments, with us coming through by ourselves, I could have sworn we won. I ran so fast with her. Whether we won our heat or not, nothing could take away the sense of victory. Something meaningful and significant had taken place. I witnessed it in others, and they witnessed it in me. Many made a point to let me know they had seen it by offering a fist-bump, a high-five, a hug, or a comment. The reality that day was greater than the vision, and this was a new vision and experience I could replay any time for inspiration.

Laying there on my back, I meditated myself back to recovery by calming my breathing, heart rate, and body, which was in a different, peacefully painful place. I felt so large laying there, as if I had just touched the hearts of all those who witnessed mine. Nothing else mattered other than I had just given myself completely. I could have been happy laying there for the rest of eternity, empty and full, with visions of life dancing through my head.

The journey had been underway for a year; the inspired vision of the book, which I aimed to stay true, was one year old. Behind it was a lifetime of vision and the collective vision of Scott and J.D., and it continued to unfold. Since our first informal meeting, countless visions guided me along the way, supporting the bigger picture.

This book is a manifestation of vision. In the beginning, I sat in a life-altering meditation. Seeds were planted and countless actions were set in motion through a powerful vision process, leading to finishing the book. I was able to see it happening. I could picture myself sitting and writing and engaging *the practice*. I could see the many steps needing to happen for the vision to unfold and for areas of my life to align.

At times, vision escaped me, which felt like losing my inner connection with God. Vision is one of our tests of faith. If we have no vision, we may be lacking faith, and paralleled with that, if we have no faith, we may either have no vision or our vision is filled with doubts. And when we lose vision, faith helps to get it back. There were periods when my vision of sitting and writing was weak and riddled with struggles. When I experienced these lulls, in a place where I couldn't see it unfolding, or when what I was seeing wasn't good, I surrendered, let go, gave it to God, released any pressure to write or finish the book, and found balance spiritually and in life.

Resting at the third eye in meditation, I would envision myself sitting and the words flowing with ease, writing my best work. I would move through to the point where the vision was vibrant and full of positive feedback. When I would then sit down to write, I would find myself back in the flow of the Universe, connected with soul purpose and fulfillment, lit up inside, and overflowing with joy. This is what I am committed to nurturing.

In the deepest way possible, I have committed myself to God and that which is greater than me – this book, the mission, my purpose, and my spiritual life. God and I made plans long before this life, and I wasn't able to find real happiness anywhere other than a heartfelt connection with God. This is all my heart truly desires. My spiritual life is where happiness lives, and sometimes nothing else matters other than simply being happy; spending years in deep-rooted spiritual depression was enough to teach me that. It has a way of changing you and hits home that happiness and living come first.

When we give our energy to growth and our faith, Divine energy and vision flow back in return. The Universe lovingly responds. This book is part of what has flowed in return, and this is also how the spiritual practice of fitness works. When you dedicate your physical practice to spiritual growth and even higher performance, you receive energy and inspired vision. You receive what you need to help you grow.

Meditative fitness is vision – clear, ongoing, and guiding. Vision lights your path as you create your life and connect with something greater. Similar to intention, vision is like a prayer that is always happening and can always be part of your practice. Vision is how we shine the light of awareness. To expand vision is to expand awareness. If a picture is worth a thousand words, then vision is worth a thousand thoughts and more. Powerful intention is found in vision, and together with these, you can work with your subconscious and program yourself to take action with ease.

We need not eyes to see. This vision happens on the inside. It has to do with our perspective, the way we see things, the way we see ourselves, our bodies, our path in life, and the world around us. Vision is linked with karma (cause and effect) and manifesting outcomes, the ability to see potential futures. It doesn't stand alone, but is connected to all, connected to the heart and senses, part intuition, part intention, awareness, and presence, part thoughts and beliefs, life experience and karma. Although we separate concepts and *the four key areas*, it is impossible to really separate that which makes us human as well as that which makes up greater vision.

Through all of our inner and outer senses, we perceive and create an image of the present moment. We can see with our eyes, or see from within; we can listen with our ears, or hear between the words and sounds; and we can touch with our skin, or feel with our heart and soul. We can see, hear, and feel more than the physical world. We have not one, but many forms of higher intelligence within ourselves and within our reach. Vision is one of them as part of *the practice*.

Life is an ongoing meditation full of vision, and we are always creating – creating our lives, our fitness, our health, and everything else. Vision resides in the creation. This is true whether we are aware of what we are creating, and it is true whether or not we guide and direct our vision. We can *go in* and create visions for ourselves, and we can also receive Divine vision.

Part of the way vision can guide you is when you pull up an image, put yourself in the vision, and observe how you feel in relation to it. It either lights you up as truth, or you realize it is not aligned with your path and will not come to fruition. And if it is something you desire from a pure heart, then you can ask, "What do I need to do for it to ring true, for it to light me up and light the way?" When we take action or realign, the way we feel in relation to the vision changes. Spend some time, especially in meditation, with thoughts and visions that light you up inside.

Darkness implies a lack of vision. When we are stuck in darkness, we are stuck in blindness, suffering, and ignorance of the truth. When we are in the light, we are happy and can see clearly, closer to Heaven on Earth.

It is possible to see things in vastly different ways. While we all have our unique perspectives, even your perspective can shift in an instant. Vision mirrors your state of being. If you are unhappy or irritable, you are at risk of seeing things in a more negative light. The lenses you see through impact the way you hear and feel, and you can see things very differently depending on whether your heart is open or closed. You can enter a meditation with a closed heart, seeing through lenses of resentment and anger, and then open your heart to see through the eyes of love and forgiveness. Is this automatic? No. It requires you to do the inner work and move through whatever is going on inside of you. *The practice* involves shifting your perspective so that you may grow.

In spiritual practice, we look within and look at ourselves to find the value and lessons in all things. We face what we need to for the purpose of growth. We take ownership over our inner world – thoughts, feelings, vision, and energy. We take ownership over our behavior, karma, and the things happening in our lives. We are not victims of our lives. We don't point fingers, judge, or blame others and our circumstances. And we also don't blame ourselves. Healthy accountability is different. If we focus only on what we do wrong and act harshly toward ourselves, we will miss it. And on the other hand, if we focus on everyone else and everything outside of ourselves, we will also miss it. We won't be engaging *the practice*. We must be aware of how we are perceiving people and the world around us. The way we see things and how we feel is never about them. At times we may need to consciously choose to be grateful and see the beauty of the world, sifting through veils of delusion and misery to the loving, caring part of us that sees the art of Earth and everyone here. We look at our judgments and see through their facade to find clarity, a higher vibration, a more enlightened life with higher vision.

We can either see through the eyes of our smaller selves or see through the eyes of God and higher self. The intention is to see clearly, to see truth and your path in life, to see yourself clearly and walk a corresponding path with your awareness. With this clarity of vision, you are able to see extensions of your karma. In spiritual practice, these aspects of vision correspond to the third-eye chakra, located at the center of your forehead. Vision found here is that of Divine intuition. It can be highly beneficial for spiritual growth and expanding vision to spend some time resting at the third eye, gazing with the Divine.

If you cannot imagine it, then how can it exist for you? You envision the life of your dreams, yet you do not believe it is possible, cannot imagine or fathom it as a truth, so you continually see your life as something else. This you can change. For more real visions, start with what you can believe in and incorporate all your senses – feeling, hearing, seeing, smelling, and tasting the vision. When you get into the art of visualization and working with the subconscious, you find there are many techniques and many ways to visualize. You can see yourself in first person looking through your own eyes, or you can observe yourself in third person from any angle. You can picture an image up close, from a distance, or on a screen. You can pull up an image of a new behavior or outcome and switch from third to first-person to help instigate the change subconsciously. You can imagine a vision within a vision, go anywhere in the world and meditate within a meditation. Relaxing visions, such as sitting on a beach watching the waves, are often used to aid relaxation in meditation. One goal in developing your vision is to create vibrant and sharp images. At the same time, it is okay if you don't see vividly. You can also sense, hear, or feel a vision intuitively; even if you can't exactly see it, you still know what it is.

For those of us who are not natural visual processors, it is a developed skill. Incorporating vision in your life can happen at any time, but one focused way to do so is through meditation. Many of the processes following these chapters involve visualization, which will help you develop your visual channel as well as create higher vision for your workouts and life. You can *go in* and create a vision with *pure intention* where there is no way for it not to be true. Not some fantasy, but a vision without limits that is real and true in your soul. The next thing you know, you find yourself doing what needs to be done for the vision to continue to be real.

Your vision helps determine what you manifest in your life. In meditation and fitness, we have great opportunities to create. We can set new goals with the vision of them being accomplished, envisioning the moment when you know you have done it. You can choose to see your body the way you want to see it. You can envision yourself shedding excess weight, watching it melt away with *pure intention* and belief. I personally know someone who lost more than 40 pounds with no changes other than meditation. Meditation and self-hypnosis for weight loss can be a powerful, effective practice, and combining it with engaging in *the workout*, consuming real food, staying hydrated, getting proper sleep, and modifying other behaviors as needed, is a strong recipe for success.

With purity of heart and intention, you can envision yourself and your life however you want as though it is already a reality. This is how you can remove subconscious blocks, plant new seeds, and program yourself for automatic change. You begin to see that you already are what your heart wants, how the vision is true right now, and you can see the karmic chain that happens for it to be true, all the things that happen along the way, the steps, the changes, discipline, and persistence – the ongoing vision. You can see that all the hows exist within the grander vision, and if needed, you can focus in on them a little closer. However, we don't necessarily need to know how it is all going to happen, only to have faith that it is happening right now, and faith that the vision will continue to unfold. We simply need the greater vision and the next step. When following the Universe in manifesting your dreams, you may not even know why you are compelled to do something until it becomes clear. This is all linked to intuition, and the questions are often simple:

How do you see yourself?

What will you allow yourself to see?

What are you willing to look at within yourself?
What will you choose to see?
Will you allow yourself to see differently?
How do you choose to view the world?
What is the vision for your life?
What are you creating for yourself?
What do you see yourself doing?
What intuitions do you have?
What will you create for yourself right now?
What is your vision?
What do you see?

You may want to read these a couple of times, three being a magic number for the subconscious to take hold. Close your eyes and allow them to sink in. The goal in *the practice* is to be willing to look at everything in order to be free and at peace. Often, the harder stuff to look at is the stuff that affects us the most. In *the practice,* we look at and release all, releasing heart and emotion until we are at peace, until we are able to look at anything about ourselves and our lives without negative reactions, but rather love and compassion. The deeply honest answers to these questions can be scary if the answers are negative. We are the common denominators of our lives and any problems or way of life we have created. I, for one, was a master of manifesting a life of depression, misery, and suffering. I failed to see good things happening in my life. If that is true for you and you don't like the life you have created or are creating, then you know something needs to change. The inner conflict provides the catalyst.

If you have doubts or difficulty imagining a life you love, you may be stuck on past behavior patterns and a past way of being, not willing to see a new possibility or believe in a new reality. With ever-expanding awareness, we can see through shallow doubts. Nothing need change outside of yourself, but simply the way you see things. When you take the first step and create a little success, you may then see the greater vision unfold.

In *the practice,* we see the karmic chain and practice mastering our karma, aligning with the positive. Karmic change happens exponentially. Much like one can slip into darkness, one can soar into the light. A slide can begin with missing a workout, then feeling down for not going, compensating with emotional eating only to feel worse, heavy and lethargic, wanting to sink or fade away into the couch. Everything becomes a chore, and before long you are farther and farther from where you wanted to be, stuck in a dark, habitual hole. What is the key to getting out of a hole? Choose to take the first or next step whether you "feel" like it or not. Stop the slide by breaking the karmic chain. Refresh your vision. No need to punish yourself. Open your heart to feel all. The way you feel, deeply and truly, is enough. Open your heart to find love, forgiveness, and grace.

Change of an upward flight works similarly in this chain reaction. You make it to *the workout,* and then choose to work on your mobility, followed by a brief meditation. With energy riding high, you eat healthy throughout the day. You have the energy to do whatever the day calls for, and later, you can sleep a deep, restful sleep, the kind that happens when you work hard and feel this good. Before you know it, you are feeling as good as you ever have, waking up strong, clear, light, and happy.

Making one small change a day can quickly amount to something measurable. If you struggle in any capacity to institute change or follow through on your intentions, look at your firsts – what you do first and what you put first. What is the first thing you do when you wake up, get to work, get home, or arrive at your workout facility? Do you find yourself in a hurry, no time for peace? What if you put being at peace first? If you are able to put first that which you would like to change, that with which you are struggling, or that which you know at the center of being matters, even for a moment, it can change the way you see things and unlock the flow of energy.

Vision as part of your preparation for *the workout* helps create your performance. Prior to a workout, envision what is to be done for the day as a form of mental practice and execution. In the sport of fitness, vision helps you plan and strategize for a specific workout. As soon as you know what the *movements* are, you pull up a vision of them, which may trigger a response within yourself. Pay attention to your reaction to ensure that you are creating what you want. Envision yourself performing with efficient, strong, flowing *movements*. Allow space for *the workout* to unfold as a meditation. Envision yourself embracing *the challenge*, pushing and exceeding prior limits, flowing from *movement* to *movement* with increasing intensity. No workout or meditation is exactly the same.

Variation applies to life and *the workout*. Repeating the same thing day after day, week after week, year after year, or workout after workout, is stagnant, shrinking energy, merely going through the motions. Challenging ourselves and trying new things expands energy and stimulates new vision.

We can either see ourselves going through *the workout* with life, passion, energy, and success, or we can see the alternative. Through vision, we can create stress, get ourselves worked up and spin out. We can create failure in advance. We may see a challenging workout and immediately envision ourselves doing poorly, or perhaps see *the workout* as a chore and dread the thought of it.

In *meditative fitness*, we are aware of what we are creating, and we choose peace and success, no matter the circumstances or outcome. The choice is yours; you can transform, mold, and shape your vision, and whenever needed, you can use inner prayer to ask and allow for renewed vision. Allow your heart and mind to align. Allow your heart to guide you to higher vision, and allow yourself to see how everything changes.

Vision helps you break limitations as you see yourself reaching new milestones, exceeding personal records, and creating new versions of yourself. *The workout* provides the opportunity. Joyous personal records can be symbolic of so much more in your heart and life. There is something special about working hard and reaching new levels, realizing you just did something that two weeks ago you could not do. This is often so special, we feel the need to share.

Recording your movement can be one of the greatest visual tools for performance, helping your vision match up with reality. How valuable is it to get a visual of your own movement versus the proper movement? It is worth more than a thought or a cue, more than a thousand words.

Vision can give you confidence in your movement, which helps you to execute. Similar to seeing over-thinking in one's movement, you can see whether someone has confidence in their movement. In *meditative fitness*, we seek to move with courage and confidence. If fears and doubts creep into the vision, pause to breathe, shake them off, and regroup to create a successful vision.

For performance, perhaps the worst thing we can do is see ourselves fail in a vision, miss a shot, a *lift*, fail a rep, or not be able to complete a workout. Sometimes these visions pop up out of nowhere, like in a flash of seeing your next golf shot slice into the woods. With developed vision, it becomes second nature to foresee the good shot, to shake off any bad visions and see success. In this way, we develop pinpoint focus, pulling up the vision and seeing it absolutely.

In visualizing your workouts, open your heart and tap into greater intention, presence, and awareness. See it all happening in an instant, without thinking, because you are in the moment, able to feel and execute with more than the physical senses. Because of your practice, because of your energy work, because of what you are creating and visualizing, you are able to sense the *movement*. You can see yourself hit a wall and keep going, reaching obstacles and overcoming. You can succeed in every vision if you choose to believe, and there is perhaps no better way to practice success.

As I finish these chapters, I sit with Allie and Stella overlooking our blessed lake. I surrender and give all to God and humanity, settling in right where I am, right where I'm supposed to be, my little place in the Universe. Everything is perfect and okay right now and always. I look to the vision of *Meditative Fitness: The Art and Practice of the Workout.* I see the book in physical form. I see athletes practicing the art in their own way. I envision you reading this, incorporating elements, using it for what works for you. I see some of you starting a meditation practice. I see others enhancing theirs. I see some of you deepening your yoga practice while others embark on new journeys of *meditative fitness.* I envision you inspiring each other and rising to greater heights. I see some using concepts to enhance their performance, and I see others using it for more fulfillment and growth in their lives. I see some of you waking up spiritually, waking up to your inner world. To you, I say welcome to your new life with new eyes.

The greater vision here doesn't end with this book. The book is part of the offering of this world of *meditative fitness* in service to all, and there will be much more to do from here, for vision is infinite in nature, no end or destination, but part of the journey, *the practice,* and life. I hope to share this with as many people as possible, whoever has an interest or desire to hear more. I see others helping to share it as well, spreading light in the world, the light of *meditative fitness* and spiritual practice.

May our success be measured by the kindness and happiness in the world, and may it be measured by the love and peace in our hearts. May we face any challenge, overcome any obstacle, and keep going with every last breath we have in us, all out of love.

My vision and prayer is that *meditative fitness* helps guide you to a more soulfully happy existence. May it represent a light on your journey. May it help you more deeply awaken spiritually, overcome challenges in your life, transform, and realize all that you are.

I believe in you. I believe in your soul. I believe in your heart and purpose. I believe in your dreams. May *meditative fitness* help you feel love in the middle of sadness and laugh and cry at the same time. May it help you to simply feel good and create a more happy and healthy being. May it help you to live with God close in your heart as you move toward the highest vision for your life.

Processes for Reference

The Processes

▲▼▲▼▲

Nothing in these pages can compare to what you can unveil within yourself through your sincere engagement of these processes. This is the precious gold of the book and what it is all about – your inner world.

These meditations are designed to help you build a *meditative fitness* practice. As you go through them, you will develop numerous techniques to apply in your life and fitness. They will help instigate growth, self-realization, and personal victories. You will have the opportunity to find answers within yourself, create visions, and peel back layers of yourself and your heart. You will work with your subconscious, make new inner connections, and create quantum change. This is where everything changes in an instant through the meditation, where your life and fitness chart a new course.

Individual processes can be completed in a short amount of time, and some techniques can even be executed in a moment. Creating *the foundation* of your practice, however, requires an initial investment of time and energy. You can do so with any amount of consistent practice. Set aside 10, 15, or more minutes to sit, align, and ground to the present moment. In those minutes, you will build the pathways of a *meditative state* – a relaxed mind, body, and central nervous system, an open heart, accessing a deeper yet more focused and alert mind. This state can be entered in an instant, in a breath, or over an extended period of time. A *meditative state* can also be entered and exited repeatedly, further relaxing and going deeper each time. With practice, you will be able to enter this state readily. In the beginning, however, it may take you a little more time as you acclimate. Be sure to give yourself grace to move through the early stages of your practice.

This *meditative state* serves as a resource before, during, and after *the workout*. It opens the gateway to new potential as you witness small miracles within yourself. In meditation, it is important not to go too deep, slowing to the point of going unconscious. Instead, you are more awake and more alert. You are not only slowing your brainwaves, but also using more of your brain. As a matter of fact, in one process, you will practice activating different areas of your brain, and overall you will practice focusing and quieting your mind, training yourself to get to a state of *pure intention.*

One of the beautiful things about meditation, self-hypnosis, and the power of your own suggestion is that you don't have to remember everything. It is not about remembering what you did and holding on to it forever, but rather the new connections that carry over into your everyday life. Spiritual growth happens at a deeper level than knowledge, and we don't have to figure it all out. Analyzing stifles the flow of energy. Rather than analyzing your meditative experiences and phenomena, it is best to take them with you into your life and ride the waves of energy.

The processes vary from sitting, standing, or walking, to going through a workout. As a universal rule in meditation and many fitness endeavors, it is important to keep a straight spine, promoting strength and alignment for the flow of energy. A straight spine helps you tune in to your body and aids your central nervous system.

When sitting, you may want to sit on a pillow or cushion with your legs crossed, or you may want to sit on the edge of a chair, rock, plyo-box, or bench. Wherever you find yourself, maintain an upright spine with a natural arch, your diaphragm lifted and open along with your chest. Your arms can rest gently on your knees, fingers natural and relaxed. Or, your arms can rest in your lap with one hand on top of the other. You may find that when your palms face down, it helps in grounding, and when your palms face up, it helps in receiving.

When standing, rest your arms gently at your sides. When relaxed, your fingers may magnetically come together to touch in a certain way. It is okay to make subtle moves as needed to get comfortable and align. It is okay to stop the meditation and re-enter. It is okay to open your eyes to read the process, then close your eyes to continue. And each time you go back in, you can delve deeper into the meditation.

Whenever you are asked whether you feel any sensations, vibrations, or energy, it is okay if you don't sense or feel anything in that moment. It is also okay if you don't have immediate answers to questions. Everything is always okay in the meditation no matter what it is – it is your meditation. Your conscious mind doesn't have to grasp everything that is happening. The awareness, rise in consciousness, and answers will come. As you grow in your practice, you will sense and feel more than before.

The processes build on each other as a progression. You will get to the point where they merge together, where you are executing a combination of them with different aspects in a single meditation, a single breath, or while moving your body, exerting yourself physically. For some of the meditations, you will be actively moving. The goal is for you to develop the meditative resources to access at any time in life or *the workout*.

The processes are also examples of different meditations. Some aspects will require practice in order to reach mastery. Once you have done one as an induction for the first time, then it becomes part of your meditative repertoire. You may go back to it at any time, refer to parts of it, repeat it for yourself, or do it quickly at a subconscious level. You can make these processes your own. Trust what you know and trust what works for you. What I want you to hear is that you have permission to trust yourself in your practice. You can trust your inner wisdom, guidance, and genius. You will know what to do, and you may be surprised as you wonder how you knew how to do that. In some meditations, you may want to use your hands and arms to help execute an intention such as releasing or clearing energy. Or you may want to accentuate a subtle sound with your breath. You will know what best helps execute your intention – when to use your hands, how to breathe, or when to accentuate little sounds. In this, be creative and take initiative. You will know when to step into your own as the master of your inner world.

If you find yourself feeling timid or silly with what you are doing in a meditation, this can prevent you from taking initiative, from trying something new, or from believing and connecting with *pure intention*. Execution requires confidence in what you are doing, and you may need to break free and let go of self-image, limiting beliefs, and judgmental thoughts. This work is more important than any of those, and we are going much deeper.

The processes work based on your sincere engagement, allowing yourself to be vulnerable. Partial effort or partial immersion will not suffice. You are what works; it is not the processes that will do your inner work for you. You will do it for you. It is all about you and what you are reflecting into your world. *The practice* becomes the mirror and shines the light. Any challenges found in meditation are an opportunity for growth. As in life, anything that happens or comes up is part of the karmic lesson. If something comes up within you, if you get frustrated with the way a process is going, or if something else is triggered, that is part of the process for you, and you must run it through until a positive shift happens.

The questions to ask are: What does this remind me of in my life? Where else have I felt this? What else is it connected to? What value can I find? Movement happens in asking the questions. Keep going until you have moved through to a better state. Grant yourself time and space to move through whatever you need to move through – give yourself grace.

Release any resistance. Surrender. Allow all things to be welcome as part of the meditation. Nothing can distract you in such a surrender. This is where pinpoint focus and expanding awareness is found, and it also means you can meditate no matter what is going on around you. You can be at peace regardless of the people, chatter, clanging of weights, music, or any other sounds. You may even find joy in all the sounds going on around you at any given time. While soft meditation music and steady sounds can be beneficial (especially early in one's practice), other noises at times may be a distracting challenge as they can get louder in your mind while meditating. You can overcome this by going through the annoyed feeling and getting to the other side. Any time an external noise bothers us, we can make peace with it from within. There is a peaceful quiet inside of you regardless of the sounds that surround you. When you find this quiet, you may find there is also music in everything. Even a leaf blower can have the ringing vibration of a bell, found at the center of the sound.

We all run our programs, do what we do, and behave in a certain way in relation to life, relationships, food, and fitness. Processing helps to interrupt patterns so that we can create new patterns, do something different, and get better results.

Processing is often a matter of asking questions. Self-processing is a matter of asking yourself questions, heightening your awareness and paying attention, listening for the answers. As a result of questions and the processing that follows, movement happens.

When questions are repeated, our answers can change as our subconscious rises to the surface. Often, at first, our answers border on taking the form of a question, as if we don't know at a surface level. Until, at some point, it clicks, the lights come on, and we have a new realization. This is what it's all about. If I were running these processes for you, I would often pause and ask you the same question many times; you would answer it many times, and your answer may either stay the same or change as you make new connections. And even when it stays the same, you can uncover more depth underneath it, more things connected to it. The question would be repeated until you have an "aha" moment.

You can read to yourself the processes that follow, or someone else can read them to you as a guided meditation. If you find your mind wandering, simply bring yourself back to the task at hand or back to the voice of your guide. Within a process, you can repeat an aspect or move on in the progression of the meditation. Questions, breaths, exercises, and techniques can be repeated at any time.

Whether you are listening to a process on audio or reading them, you set the pace. You can pause to allow more time whenever needed. In any process, you can follow where it leads you. You can detour and come back to it. You can flow with the meditation and see where it takes you.

Many of the processes are active meditations. A beautiful union of active and passive meditation can be found by pausing on an aspect at any time, simply to be and enjoy the precious moments, observing your thoughts, intuitions, intentions, feelings, sensations, vibrations, energy, *the breath, the body,* and vision. When you sense or feel a particular vibration, you can go into the vibration to strengthen and expand it. This is your practice, and you will be familiarizing yourself with your inner world and your unique meditative phenomena, familiarizing yourself with what it feels like for you to relax, for you to reach *pure intention,* and for you to find a meditative brainwave. Once familiar, you will know when you are there. You will find the tools to build and enhance your practice in what follows. The processes hold the keys to *meditative fitness* and infinite possibilities.

The Foundation

Meditative Fitness Induction

WELCOME TO THE initiation into your practice. In this process, you will take a look at and set your intentions and outcomes. These are best framed in the positive, for your subconscious doesn't recognize the negative. For example, you would not want to say, "Stop being lazy." The subconscious hears, "Being lazy." Instead, you might say, "Live an active and vibrant life." Whatever answers arrive, frame them in the positive. Examples could range from the smallest steps to the grandest of visions: making it to the gym, cooking a meal, practicing a certain number of times per week, or creating more peace, love, joy, or happiness in your life. They could be about hitting personal records in your workouts or competing in an event. Whatever they are, they are uniquely yours.

These are not things you <u>have</u> to do, but things you <u>want</u> to do. Connect with your underlying intentions that are already present. It is already who you are with higher intentions waiting to spark into action. It is your path of fulfillment and soul bliss. Sometimes life has to appear bad enough for us to see and choose this path, and we can always stay right where we are. Perhaps the worst thing we can do is set goals only to get down on ourselves for not following through, which is a good formula for getting more stuck than we were previously. You will likely encounter an impasse if they are overwhelming, appear to be beyond reach, or if you don't fully believe in them. On the simplest level, one goal could be to start your practice by engaging in your first conscious meditative workout. When you reach that one, then you set the next one and so on, all leading to the greater vision. Set yourself up for success and infinite possibilities. As long as you can see and believe, then it is well within your reach. If you can't see it, then you may simply need to take some steps to be able to see it.

For each question, close your eyes, take a deep breath, focus on relaxing into yourself, ask the question, pause, and breathe while receiving the answer from within. It is also okay if you don't get immediate conscious answers. Your subconscious will hear you. Something deeper and greater within will hear you. Questions can be repeated silently or aloud as needed until answers materialize. Questions can be repeated individually, or the entire list of questions can be repeated for as long as you would like, or until you know you are done – when you have a new realization or light-bulb moment. If you like, you can write down your answers, however, it is not required. Nothing, in fact, is required. This is all for you, guilt-free. Feel free to do with it what you will. Are you ready for something significant in your life? Engage this with sincerity and create your experience.

Find a comfortable place to sit or stand.

Close your eyes, take a deep breath, in through your nose, hold it at the top before slowly letting it go out through your mouth.

Feel your mind and body relax while your breath falls. Repeat as necessary until you are ready to continue. Now, ask yourself...

What does your practice symbolize to you?

What does it mean to you at a deeper level?

What all is it connected to?

For what reasons will you engage in your practice?

What in your life would you like to be better?

How would you like to feel?

What do you want for your body?

Your heart? Your mind? Your spirit?

What are your goals? What results are you seeking?

What outcomes would you like?

What are the highest intentions for your practice?

Open your eyes, take some more deep breaths with slow exhales.

Now repeat the following until you know you are done, when you feel a positive shift or rise in vibration.

These are my intentions.

These are my goals.

This is my life, and it is happening.

These are my highest intentions.

These are my highest goals.

This is my life, and it is happening right now.

I am reaching my goals, dreams, and pure hearted desires.

Repeat the last statement twice more and pay attention to any thoughts and feelings that come up when you make that declaration. Pay attention to your belief, whether it resonates with truth and strength and whether you can see it happening. Now that you have gone through those questions, take a moment to let it all sink in.

Close your eyes and see everything, all your answers and anything else swirling around, wrap it all up, and create an image in your mind.

How do you see yourself when you are reaching your goals and living your dreams? What do you see yourself doing? How do you know you are living your dreams? What triggers that knowledge? A feeling inside, a confirmation from the Universe? What happens that says you are doing it? What do you see, hear, smell, taste, touch, and feel?

Pull up the image now. Allow everything to be part of your vision. What do you see yourself eating or drinking or putting into your body? Can you see the planning that goes into it? What discipline, dedication, and determination do you see? When do you see yourself engaging in your workouts? What intentions are you setting? Can you see yourself meditating? If so, when? What is your daily spiritual prescription for yourself? How much can you see all at once? Can you see all of the things that support your intentions and goals? Can you see how it is all part of the journey? How does it feel? How does it feel to be living that way? What masterpiece of a loving life are you creating, and what else will you create with your practice? See it now. And enjoy that which you are creating, enjoying the process, enjoying the journey.

From that point in time where you know you are living it, look back on all the steps you took to get there. What has helped you along the way? Can you see the points when you slipped or took detours? What did you do? What did you do to get back up after falling? How did you take the first step out of a slide, back toward your mountain top?

Going back to your image of success, you can spend as much time with it as you would like. And when you are ready, bring yourself back into your present time and space, and open your eyes, fully present and awake.

Intention-Check

Close your eyes, take a deep breath, relax, and ask yourself:

What do you believe you are capable of?

Do you limit yourself?

If you can't see it happening, is it possible for you?

Or would it simply be an accident if it were to be realized?

How powerful are you to either manifest or block your intention?

How strong is your intention?

How strong are your doubts and counter-intentions?

When you say you are going to do something, do you do it?

What false realities are you constructing?

Do your words match up with your actions?

How strong is your intention in your workouts?

How do you feel upon completing your workouts?

How strong is your will, focus, and purpose in action?

What are you creating? What will you create?

What are your highest intentions?

What would it be like to know?

To know who you are. To know what you believe.

To know where you are headed in your life.

It is only a matter of uncovering your truth.

Again, what are your highest intentions?

With a deep, intention-filled breath, open your eyes.

The Art of Relaxation

If all you ever did was practice the art of relaxation, it would be a beautiful and beneficial practice. This process focuses on a foundation of relaxation from which to build on, and it opens the doors to *pure intention*, becoming your breath, and tuning in to your body. In this process, however, we are simply focusing on the art of relaxing, which helps you to enter a *meditative state* and tap into your parasympathetic functioning. You can apply this skill any time throughout your days or workouts. In this process you are not manipulating your breath. Instead, use your natural breath to help you relax. Allow it to become a calming wave as it rises and falls.

Find a comfortable space to sit or stand with a straight vertical spine.

Close your eyes, take a deep breath, and immediately begin to relax.

With each moment that passes, you will continue to relax yet remain wide awake. Allow all else to float away – any thoughts, worries, and anything happening in your life. Let it all float away, even if only for a moment. All there is to do right now is relax. Nothing else but relax. If you need to, make an inner gesture to offer up anything that is lingering.

Now, tighten your muscles and your body, then release and allow yourself to further relax, feeling the contrast. Notice the tension that arises as your inhale reaches its capacity, then relax further with each exhale. Shake your hands and arms to loosen any tension and allow for deeper relaxation. Starting with the top of your head and forehead, relax. Relax all muscles and release any tension from your face. Relax the inside of your mouth down to your throat and feel the difference of the air passing through a relaxed passageway. Relax under your skin. Release any inner pressure. Relax your neck and shoulders down to your chest and heart. Feel the melting, dispersing, and floating away of any tension. Relax your abdomen and inner organs, allowing them to function with ease. Relax your arms and hands, and notice the relaxation is contagious, catching on everywhere your consciousness travels. Allow the relaxation to spread to your hips, thighs, legs, calves and shins, all the way down to your feet and toes. Relax anywhere there is tension or foreign energy, down to the last cell in your body. Expand and relax your entire body all at once, as though your body is singing a song of relaxation, sitting or standing there completely relaxed. Notice any vibrations.

You may want to set a reminder for this state, an *anchor* for relaxation. What could you do to remind yourself of and to help you enter this state? It could be when your fingers touch a certain way. It could be a certain type of breath. It could simply be when you close your eyes. What will you use to remind yourself and help you to relax in a moment or a single breath? Practice it now, and continue to practice the art of relaxation for as long as you would like.

When you are ready, take a deep breath, gather your energy, right here, right now, fully present and awake, and open your eyes.

Becoming the Breath

This process involves a series of different types of breaths, each of which could also be separate meditations. As you go through this process, give yourself a little time with each type of breath and observe the different sensations. Take your time. Working with your breath is a worthwhile investment as one of the keys to many possibilities. These breathing skills can also be used at any time in one's day or workout. Working with your breath greatly enhances your ability to relax, work with your energy, recover and perform in your workouts, and much more. This is about you developing your practice with your breath. You will determine what works best for you, which can also change as your practice grows.

Find a comfortable place to sit with a straight spine.

Close your eyes, take a deep breath, and relax.

Focus all of your awareness on your breath. Starting with a natural breath, observe the rise and fall. This is also where you learn to watch your thoughts. If your mind wanders, bring yourself back to your breath.

Take a deep breath in and hold it for a second before slowly releasing it, relaxing with the fall. Exhale all the way out and again hold for a moment before breathing back in. With each breath, you will continue to relax into a deeper state of being, relaxed yet awake, alert, and focused. Begin to count your breaths for a moment. Each inhale and exhale is one breath. As long as you are able to count, you will know you haven't gone too deep. When you reach five, go back to simply observing the rise and fall of your breath.

Now, focus on breathing up and down your body. With each inhale, breathe your attention and awareness from your feet up to the top of your head, and with each exhale breathe from the top of your head down to your feet and the ground below. Do this for five or more breaths. You are programming your ability to scan your body.

When you are ready, move to the length of your spine, and begin to breathe up and down your spine. With each inhale, breathe up from the base of your spine to the top of your head. You may find your spine lifting, lengthening, and aligning. You can continue for as long as you like and practice this regularly to tap into the currents of energy along your spine.

Next, test a couple of breaths at different speeds, focusing simply on how quickly, smoothly, or slowly you are breathing, still up and down your spine, connecting and anchoring in your breath, tapping into your central nervous system. When you are ready, on your next breath, rest your attention in the area of your neck, head, and forehead. Breathe smoothly and naturally with your consciousness resting in this area. Continue to notice your breathing. You are always able to be aware, always observing, even when you are not paying attention to this observance. Notice any vibrations that are present, simply noticing what you feel.

Now, place your hand on your stomach. As you breathe in, breathe from your abdomen with the air pushing your belly out against your hand. Stop your inhale when the air fills your abdomen, breathing only from your diaphragm without involving your chest. This can take some practice.

Next, start your breath in your stomach, first filling your abdomen and then expanding to your chest, taking in as much air as possible. When it doesn't feel like you can take in any more, expand a little more, all the way up to your throat. On the exhale, release and allow the air to flow out, and when you don't think you can exhale any more, contract and push out every last bit of air, fully contracting the muscles that aid your breath. This is an exercise of expanding and strengthening your lungs. Spend a few moments with some natural *core breaths*, no additional force or effort required other than starting and ending *the breath* from your diaphragm, breathing deeply at the core of being.

Next, find *the breath* that best promotes relaxation for you. Find *the breath* that feels best to you. With a little practice, you may automatically go to *the breath* that best serves the moment.

On your next breath, inhale deeply, slower than normal, and exhale even slower and longer than the inhalation. Test how long and slow you can take one breath, from 30-60 seconds or more. Practice breathing as slowly as you can without feeling a loss of oxygen. Once you have had some fun with that, find your perfect breath for this moment. Focus on your breath and every aspect of it. How does it feel? What does it sound like? What do you hear? Focus on the energy of your breath and the connection between it and the energy of your body. See if you can notice the flow of energy. Notice any sensations throughout your body, simply paying attention. Notice any vibrations that are present. Can you feel the molecules in motion? If not, that is okay. What do you feel? This is where you start.

Now return to a natural state of breathing, simply allowing your breath to be. Breathe naturally in through your nose and out through your mouth. Focus on the air coming through your nose and down, then passing back out through your throat, mouth, and lips. Next, breathe in and out through your mouth. Focus on the air passing your lips, mouth, and throat, filling your chest and abdomen before leaving again, passing through your airway and across your lips. Where does your breath end and you begin?

What does it feel like to be one with your breath? What does it feel like to become your breath? Continue to notice the air that fills and leaves your lungs. You may continue on in this way for as long as you like and see what happens. Experiment with different methods of breathing out through your mouth, with different subtle sounds being made based on the size of the opening and the speed of the air that passes. When you are ready, take one more deep breath, gathering all of your energy to where you now sit, fully present and awake, and open your eyes.

Different ways of breathing can help execute intentions in meditation. In future processes, you will practice releasing energy with your breath. You will practice additional locational breathing in your *body*. You will practice creating strength, accessing your heart, and more, one breath at a time. For now, connecting and becoming your breath is the beginning.

One Breath

Whenever you slow within yourself and slow your brainwaves, you are meditating. This can happen in any moment in time, and your breath can help you to do so. For this process, simply practice one meditative breath at a time. Start with a natural, deep, relaxing breath, and begin to add intention one breath at a time. Close your eyes, take a deep meditative breath, and open your eyes. Practice relaxing in one breath, releasing specific tension in one breath, going to a deeper state of being, activating more of your brain, creating or gathering strength in one breath, breathing the length of your body in one breath. For one breath at a time, you may practice any type of intention-filled breath.

As you progress, practice these one breath meditations with your eyes open and in your workouts as well.

Breath Strength Vision

Close your eyes, take a deep breath, and relax.

As you settle into a deeper state of being, going deeper with each breath, imagine your breath as life and energy. Imagine that your breath is your strength and power. Allow yourself to create a vision in your mind's eye. Within this vision, you open your eyes and look around to find yourself in an open space. The darkness of what seems like night extends for infinity, yet somehow you are still able to see. With no sound other than your thoughts, what does it feel like to be in this space? What do you do? Intuitively, you sense a direction, and you begin to walk. Before long you come to a giant stone wall, extending up and to the sides as far as the eye can see. This wall stands in your way, and somehow you know that you must get to the other side. You look around, taking it all in, looking for anything that could possibly help. That's when you see it. High above your head there is a spot in the wall, and a little ray of light shines through. This tells you two things. There is light on the other side, and the wall is not impenetrable. What does this light represent to you? Will you allow yourself to believe? There is nothing around to help you get through, so you look to the only place left. You look within yourself. You know you must gather all of your strength to move this wall. You take a deep breath, gathering every bit of strength you have in you, and powerfully exhale, WHOOSH! Send the air out with everything you have, hands extended in front of you, palms toward the wall, as though you are breathing with all of your being out of your mouth and hands with the *pure intention* of moving the wall. You are using your arms and hands and entire body and being. You repeat the process, deep summoning breath, and WHOOSH! The wall starts to give. It moves a clear foot with each breath as your strength and belief increase. You ask yourself, "If I can move a wall with the strength of my breath, what else can I do?" The wall is still there, still between you and the light and everything good. On the next breath, you set the intention for the wall to come down. You close your eyes and envision the wall crumbling or disintegrating, turning to dust in front of you. Take a deep breath, connect with *pure intention*, and exhale with the perfect breath, perfect frequency and vibration, and watch the wall fall like sand in front of you, revealing a beautiful radiant light unlike any you have seen before, as though the sky and space are glowing with oranges and yellows. Unlike the sun, here you can gaze directly into the light. It appears to shine right through you, connecting with and cleansing every cell. You stand there, basking in this moment and in the light. What does it feel like to be connected to this light? Take a deep breath and soak it all in. Spend as long as you want here, and from here, you can go wherever you want.

When you are ready, bring yourself back to where you are, back within yourself, fully present and awake, and open your eyes.

Tuning in to the Body

As a key element of *the foundation*, this practice is about tuning in to your body – including your heartbeat, heart rate, energy, breathing, and any other pulses, vibrations, or sensations through-out your body. You will practice locational breathing, moving your attention and awareness within your body, and focusing on the space your body occupies, familiarizing yourself with your space.

Find somewhere to sit or stand with a straight spine.

Close your eyes, take a deep breath in, and pause briefly at the top before slowly letting it out. Survey your body as your breath falls. As you settle in, going deeper with each breath, focus on the space you occupy.

Where does this space extend to?

What is this space connected to?

What do you sense?

Where does your consciousness reside?

Where is the consciousness of your body?

Where is the center of your being?

Where is the center of every cell?

Focus on the space you occupy and sense all that you can.

Take a moment to acknowledge all the signals being sent throughout your body. Your body is always working, seeking harmony.

With each breath, run the length of your body. Starting your breath and attention at your feet and toes, inhale all the way up to the top of your head, then exhale back down your body, through your feet and into the earth, then rising up again. As you do this, scan your body and the flow of energy. Are there any areas that need extra love and care? After a few scanning breaths, pause with your attention resting at the base of your spine, the area of your tailbone, and spend some time breathing from there.

Next, move up to below your belly button and spend some time breathing there. Now, move up and spend some time in your abdomen.

Continue to your heart and chest, your throat, the back of your neck, your forehead, and the top of your head. Practice breathing and spending time in each of these areas. Notice the energy of each area and how it feels, any sensations, thoughts, or messages.

Next, expand to the entire space of your body and return to a natural breath. Focus on the space in which your body resides. Take your time and practice sensing your entire body all at once.

What do you feel in this space?

What does it feel like?

How do you envision this space?

What does the energy feel like?

How is your energy flowing?

Are there any areas that need to be cleared?

Is there any tension to be relaxed?

Continue to focus on this space and simply observe – observe your breath, your heartbeat, heart rate, and any other pulses or sensations throughout your body. Allow the entire space of your body to breathe. What will you radiate from this space?

Continue to practice tuning in to your body for as long as you wish. You can deepen and expand this practice, and you can return to it at any time, with your eyes open or closed, tuning in, sensing your space. You have always had this skill and awareness, and you will always be able to access it. For now, when you are ready, fully present and alert, open your eyes.

Mind, Body, Heart, Soul

In this process, we will spend some time in your heart, mind, body, and soul, each of which could be separate meditations. A shorter version would be to simply spend a little time in each area then expand and meld them together as one.

Find a space to sit with a straight spine.

Close your eyes, take a deep breath, and relax.

Practice flowing your attention and energy up with your exhales.

After a few long breaths, move your attention to the base of your spine and breathe the length of your spine, in and up from your seat to the top of your head, and back down. Again, practice flowing up with your exhales. Withdraw your energy to your spine and practice flowing within.

On your next breath, pause when you reach the back of your neck. After a moment, move to your forehead, and expand to the entire space of your brain. With all attention focused on this space, imagine a door in the middle. This is the door to your greatest potential. This is the door to the full capacity of your mind, your truth, inner wisdom and genius. Open the door to access more of your mind. You are moving to a deeper state of awareness, activating more of your brain.

For an added bonus, with your fingertips, gently tap a loving, healing intention. Tap your temples, down and around your eyes and cheeks, up to your forehead, and all around your head, anywhere that feels right.

With your attention on your forehead, imagine you are firing signals, neurons, and synapses, lighting up your brain. Imagine them like little lightning bolts. Move to your left brain and light it up. Then move to your right brain and fire the signals. Next, move to the back of your brain light it up. Now the back of your neck, your medulla region, and fire signals. Notice any sensations, then expand to light up the entire space of your brain.

Moving on to your heart, on your next breath, move to the center of your chest and pause with your consciousness resting in this area. Gently tap your sternum to help open and awaken the energy of your heart. What do you feel in this moment? What is in your heart? What is under the surface? Does anything need to be released? Take a moment to simply feel what you feel. Acknowledge and surrender to your truth in this. Imagine a small dot in the center of this space. With each breath, expand the dot, expand the circle and radiate from your heart. You may want to hum, sing, or let out a little sound from this center. Notice any sensations, vibration, or emotion. What touches your heart or moves you? Go with it and go into it, feeling all that may accompany it. What does it feel like to experience the world with an open heart? Here is where you can move through any feelings that arise, face anything, sit with strength in your feelings, and harness all of your heart energy. Spend as long as you like here and revisit often.

When you are ready, expand your consciousness to your entire body and the space it occupies. This is your space. Focus on feeling and envisioning the space in which you sit. Envision your silhouette. Envision it from within yourself. Associate with this silhouette. With an open heart and mind, what do you have for your body in this moment?

What does your body have for you?

What is it responding to?

What does your body allow you to do?

What does it allow you to experience?

How can you be more loving toward your body?

What does your body want?

What do your heart and mind want for your body?

You can repeat these questions as you wish to elicit new connections, and as always, you may spend as long as you like in this union, melding your heart, mind, and body together as one.

Now, bring your attention to your soul. What do you sense about the soul of who you are? Focus on the life and energy that animates your body. Focus on something greater within, all of your magnificence underneath all else. Strip away external circumstances, past behaviors, future worries, and all of the things pulling at you in life. See if you can sense your soul's perfection. See if you can connect with soul bliss. See if you can hear the song of your soul. See if you can sense the journey of your soul. Listen and pay close attention to anything that comes to you in these moments. What is here for you in these moments? What do you know from deep within? How does your soul influence your heart, mind, and body?

Move your attention back to your heart, mind, and body. Imagine all of them coming together, merging with your soul. Feel them aligning to work together toward your greatest good. There is no more conflict, only peace, bliss, and fulfillment. You can be free within yourself no matter the circumstances. Take a moment to create an image of life in this way for you. What does it look like for you? Program this image with *pure intention*. This is your life and your soul's journey.

You may spend as much time as you want creating this image. You can also revisit any part of this process, giving extra attention where needed or continuing to integrate and unite them all. When you are ready, fully present and awake, sitting right where you are, open your eyes.

Grounding and Expanding

Focusing inward, we can also maintain awareness of our surroundings and the outside world. We can expand this awareness as far as our consciousness will allow. This process is about cultivating this presence and awareness. In this process, like the others, you may repeat any of these breaths or move on in the progression to the next breath, and you may pause at any time simply to be with your presence and awareness.

Find a comfortable place to sit or stand with a straight spine.

Close your eyes, take a deep breath in, and relax.

Start by grounding to the present moment. What do you sense? What do you hear, see, smell, taste, and feel? What do you feel in your heart? What sounds are going on around you? Invite all as part of your experience, all as part of the meditation. What does the air feel like around you, filling your lungs? What does the space feel like where you are sitting? With your breath, gather all of your energy into your body. You are right here, right now. Take a deep breath in, gathering all energy from around you and above you, and on the exhale, allow this energy to flow down through your feet to the center of the Earth, of what you imagine the center of Earth to be, then allow it to flow back up to rest within. You are rooted right where you are, grounded. Any time you gather energy within yourself and bring yourself into focus and into the present moment, you are grounding in presence. You may repeat these grounding breaths as desired.

Bring your awareness to any sensation or vibration that is present. You may take a moment to go into, strengthen, and expand any such vibration. Focus your attention inward while still noticing and observing all that is going on around you, including little sounds and movements in your surroundings. You are developing pinpoint focus with expanding awareness. Bring this focus to your breath and any vibration that is present.

On your next in-breath, again gather energy from all around you. On the exhale, ground this energy, flowing through your feet to the earth. On your next inhale, flow up with the energy through your feet, expanding your awareness and energy to fill the space of your body. Allow your consciousness and energy to fill this space.

From here, flow into another deep grounding breath, grounded within yourself. In unison with long breaths, as long as needed to ground and expand, flow and expand to a couple of feet around your body. Envision this space before returning to an energy-gathering inhale, a grounding exhale, then flow and expand your awareness to the room or surrounding area that you are in. Notice any sensations, sounds, or movement, aware of this entire space. Envision this space. Sense this space and feel the energy.

From here, flow back to an energy-gathering inhale, bringing your energy within yourself, rooted right where you are, then flow back up and send your awareness, energy, and vibration further than before, perhaps a building or other large surrounding space. Observe this awareness and energy, filling the entire space. Now return to another energy-gathering, grounding breath before flowing back up and extending to a larger area, your neighborhood, town, or city. Add an intention of love and peace, and radiate this with your awareness. Expand your awareness and vision to this space, sending your energy and vibration before grounding again. Continue to repeat this process, expanding out to your state, country, and continent, all the way to encompass our planet and the Universe. Expand as far as your consciousness will allow.

Once you are finished alternating between grounding and expanding, focus all of your attention and awareness on the center of your heart. Still focusing on your center, expand your awareness beyond yourself, again progressing to the Universe. Spend some time resting with this inner presence and expanding awareness.

When you are ready, fully conscious, fully present, grounded and awake, sitting or standing where you are, open your eyes.

For an added bonus, with your eyes open, practice focusing on a specific spot and expand your vision and attention to your peripherals while still looking at the spot you have chosen. Take in as much visually as you can, noticing anything that moves, then practice expanding all around you, out into the Universe, seeing all around you and beyond.

Pure Intention Vision

Find a comfortable place to sit or stand.

Close your eyes, take a deep breath in, and relax with the fall.

Allow yourself to create a vision in your mind's eye. You are about to go somewhere that will allow you to run freely, somewhere with an open space, somewhere that helps you feel free. Where will you go? Where will you go to find *pure intention*? If you could go anywhere to do this, where would it be? When you have it, envision yourself standing, closing your eyes, and when you open them within the vision, you will be in this place. Go there now. What do you see? What is the landscape? What do you see in the horizon? What do you sense? What is your intuition? What do you hear? What do you smell, taste, and feel? What does the ground feel like under your feet? This is where you will run. Turn to face your runway. What do you see? Describe it to yourself or your guide for more of the vision to unfold. Are there any trees around? Are there any mountains nearby or bodies of water, perhaps a pond, a creek, river, lake, or ocean? Are there any obstacles on your path? Are there any obstacles within yourself? If so, how will you overcome them? How will you push past any physical, mental, or emotional challenges? How will you override those circuits?

Now facing your path, you are about to run. This beautiful space has been chosen for a higher purpose. As you face your runway, you close your eyes and envision running to see how far and fast you can run without slowing down. What are you running toward? What does this run represent to you? What is waiting for you on the other side?

You begin to run smoothly, feeling light and good on your feet, breathing to match the pace. Something clicks. It feels so good to be moving, you increase in speed until you are flying as fast as you can, each foot barely touching as you glide across the ground. There is no finish line in sight until you decide to slow down and stop, but all you want to do is keep flying toward your highest potential. You go from feeling good to feeling everything that comes with maximum exertion. The physical sensations take over your body. What does it feel like to you? Notice the inner dialogue as you survey your body in motion. At a certain point, you will consider slowing down. How much further could you possibly go? Hard to know. Will you talk yourself into slowing down? No.

You are still sprinting, beginning to think there is no way you can go much further, but *pure intention* overrides, and you continue flying, feeling the wind against your skin. You do not resist the burning in your lungs, but rather embrace and continue breathing the best you can. Your mind and body have surrendered to your heart and intention. You access something inside that propels you to keep going despite anything else. *Pure intention* leads the way and nothing else matters, not your thoughts, not your legs, not the physical sensations, only the strength of your will.

Still sprinting, barely able to keep going, and still you continue a little further, and a little further, and a little further, and you know you have just done something significant, pushing beyond what you thought possible, beyond prior conceived limits. Your intention carries you through.

When you decide to, you begin to slow down to a jog, then a walk, then standing still, recovering your breath and energy. Within moments, your breathing and heart rate relax. Your chest is open as you stand straight and tall. Take a look around from where you now stand. Has anything changed in your scenery or the way you see the world? Still in the vision, you close your eyes. You began this run in meditation and you will end this run in meditation. After some time, when you are ready, you look around at all the sights one last time, soaking in this special place. You can come back here whenever you want to spend some time, to meditate, go for a run, or practice flying. For now, though, it is time to return from this place. Bring yourself back to where you now sit or stand, fully present, fully awake, and open your eyes.

Water Intention

This simple practice can be applied whenever you drink water. It is especially beneficial around your workouts, before and after meditation or soft-tissue mobility work, as well as before bed and upon waking up.

Start with intuitive awareness. Like a small admission to yourself, the intention represents your honest, heart-level, vulnerable choice, the conscious direction of your life. The important thing is to connect sincerely with your intention. Examples may include love, peace, joy, forgiveness, energy, clarity, cleansing, or healing. This process can be done with your eyes open or closed, and you can reach the point where it happens subconsciously whenever you drink water. You will need a glass or bottle of water, preferably cold to heighten the inner sensation.

Holding the glass with both hands, take a deep relaxing breath.

Send the intention of your choice into the water, and then drink.

Feel the inner sensation of the water and intention flooding in.

And repeat as desired.

For an added bonus, add intention in unison with your exhale, and imagine the intention emanating from your heart through your hands, or from above, through the top of your head, and into your hands. Ask for what you need from a place of surrender within yourself.

Belief Awareness

Find a comfortable place to sit or stand.

Close your eyes, take a deep breath in, and relax with the fall.

It is time to connect with something greater within yourself, a part of you that will always have the answer to your truth at any moment in time. Spend a little time breathing with each question. Your beliefs will be with you at every stage of your practice.

What do you believe about yourself?

What do you believe about your life?

Not what you want to believe, not the story you tell yourself.

Test and check yourself and your beliefs.

What is behind the stories and what you want to believe?

What do you really believe under the surface?

What are your subconscious beliefs?

What are you willing to acknowledge?

Are your beliefs limiting in any way? How do you limit yourself?

Are you willing to change or expand what you believe?

What false beliefs do you need to release?

Remove all limitations.

What now do you believe about yourself and your life?

What do you truly believe? And where do you place your faith?

When you are ready, present with your faith, open your eyes.

Energy Clearing

In this process, we will go through some simple methods of clearing energy, adding a new layer to *the foundation*, building on becoming *the breath* and tuning in to *the body*. Applications include daily meditations, preparation for *the workout,* and mobility work such as stretching or foam rolling, which is where you can practice clearing the energy along with the soft tissue release. Some of the techniques include breathing energy, moving and expanding energy, working with the vibration of energy, spinning energy, and exchanging energy.

Find a comfortable place to sit or stand.

Close your eyes, take a deep breath in, and relax with the fall.

Begin by tuning in to the energy of your breath and body. Scan your body, breathing up and down. Notice the flow of energy and any sensations or vibrations. Bring your awareness to the subtle energies in and around your body. Are there any areas that feel as though they need to be cleared? Where would you like to give some extra love and care? When you have your answer, begin to breathe in and out from that location. Wherever it is, it is breathable. The energy can flow in and out from wherever you choose. With each exhale, allow any undesired energy to flow out of your energy field. With each inhale, allow clear, awake, loving and healing energy to flow inward, cleansing from within, aiding the next breath to continue to clear the energy. Keep going in this way until you feel the energy change.

Next, as you breathe in, gather any undesired energy within you and allow it to flow up and out with your breath, through your heart, throat, forehead, and the crown of your head. Do this with *pure intention*.

If you sense a vibration anywhere in your body, it can be helpful in clearing energy. With each breath, go into the vibration. Focus intently on expanding the vibration, making it as big as you can. Move the vibration throughout your body to clear a particular location.

On your next breath, move your consciousness to a new area to be cleared, perhaps your stomach, heart, throat, head, or anywhere you feel abnormalities or disharmony. Using all of your faculties (vision, hearing, and feeling), imagine encircling and spinning the energy like a funnel – swoosh, swoosh, swoosh. Create a unique sound in your mind or at a whisper to aid the process and serve as an *anchor* for the future. Continue to spin the energy with each breath, building up speed as you exhale, spinning the energy up and out, clearing the space. Spin the energy up from the area, up from your stomach, heart, throat, head, and through the crown of your head. Repeat and continue until you feel the energy change, then fill yourself with the positive energy of your choice until you are overflowing, sending that energy out into the world to balance the energy you let go.

When you are ready, reground your energy within yourself, clear and fully present, and open your eyes.

For an added bonus, use your hands to brush off your energy field or to symbolically pull or release energy from a particular location. This might look like brushing off your shoulders, head, neck, arms, torso, and legs. It might look like rubbing an area to create a sensation to work with. It might look like touching a location with your fingers together as though you are reaching in to free the space. As always, find what works best for you.

Heart Clearing

You can open and engage your heart in any workout or meditation. You can spend some time in your heart when you experience heightened love and gratitude or any other emotion. In future processes, we will practice magnetizing and making these bigger. We will expand on engaging and opening your heart in relation to your workouts. This process, however, is about clearing the feelings lurking underneath that often cause turmoil and surface-level conditions such as anger, irritability, anxiety, and even depression. This is about the emotions that drive your behavior from under the surface. It is a process of surrender and release. You can engage in this process when something touches your heart or when you are struggling with inner conflict. You will know when it is time to surrender.

Find a comfortable place to sit or stand.

Close your eyes, take a deep breath in, and relax with the fall, falling into the realm of your heart.

First, with one of your hands, tap your fingertips against your sternum. Then, place your hands together prayer-like in front of your chest; gently tap the back of your thumbs against your chest. Pay attention to what is going on within you. Move your hands, still together, from your heart up to your forehead. Slightly bow your head and touch your thumbs to your forehead. This alone is an act of vulnerability and surrender. Will you let your guard down? With your hands back against your heart, notice how when you bow your head, your fingertips reach up to your lips and nose. Raise your hands slightly so that your fingers rest on the bridge of your nose as your lips touch your thumbs. Rising a little more, your thumbs rest on your nose with your fingers on your forehead, all of these like puzzle pieces that fit together. These simple gestures carry inherent intention. When you are ready, release your hands to your preferred position.

Imagine yourself traveling from your head down to your heart.

With each breath, tune in to your heart.

What touches your heart? What moves you?

What do you feel? What do you feel right now, in this moment?

What is the overwhelming feeling under the surface?

Have you been denying yourself from feeling anything?

What will you admit to yourself, and what will you let go and let out?

It is your job to ping your own heart.

It may take a little time as you tune in and open your heart.

Is there anything weighing on you? What is calling to be released?

There are many layers of your heart to peel back.

Surrender to the truth of what you feel, and keep going.

Go into these feelings and focus on feeling them fully.

The deeper the surrender, the more you may need to release. You may need to continue to release for some time to move through all of it, and you may need to repeat in waves. You are doing this work to leave yourself in a better place, at peace. When the surrender happens, you are able to feel love, peace, and joy, as well as whatever else you are releasing. You are able to feel the entire scope of emotions. Continue to move through and allow yourself to feel the light and good that is here for you in these moments.

And when you are ready, fully present with an open heart, sitting or standing right where you are, open your eyes.

Pre-Workout

Intention Setting

THIS IS A process of setting intention for your workouts, which can happen at any time leading up to and even during a workout, and it can happen in an instant. The specific intention is personal to you. It could be related to problems you are facing as a request for clarity. It could be related to your heart and feelings; mental health; your body and fitness goals; or your faith, soul fulfillment, and spiritual life.

Find a comfortable place to sit or stand.

Close your eyes, take a deep breath in, and relax with the fall.

Tune in to your heart, mind, body, and spirit. Tune in to your breath and energy. Tune in to where you are right now.

What do you feel in your heart?

What do you sense in your body?

What kind of energy is present?

What thoughts are going through your mind?

What would you like to improve?

What questions would you like to have answers to?

What problems would you like to have solutions for?

How do you want to feel at the end of your workout?

What kind of thoughts and energy would you like to have?

What does your workout represent to you today?

What intention will you put into your workout?

Wrap all of this up and declare it to yourself, framing it in the positive. Create a vision of the intention. Allow yourself to believe your intention is both possible and inevitable. This is where you will be by the end of your workout. How do you see yourself engaging *the workout* to get there? Resting your awareness at your forehead, focus with *pure intention*. Spend a moment gazing with pinpoint focus at the vision you have created. It is real and true right now. After a moment, move your attention to a deeper space in your brain. Imagine a level wave running through the middle of your brain. You are placing the intention in your subconscious, programming it for automatic execution. Repeat the intention either silently or aloud to yourself, letting it sink in. The intention has been set in motion; the seed has been planted.

When you are ready, take a deep breath and open your eyes.

Dedicating the Practice

Similar to setting intentions, you can also dedicate your practice and workouts. This dedication may be related to an intention or it may not. Although the act of dedication requires intention, the dedication itself isn't always an intention, but rather an object of the intention. You can dedicate your practice and workouts to anything in alignment with higher purpose and goodness. You may dedicate it to loved ones, others in the gym, or for the benefit of all. You may dedicate it to your faith, happiness, or a higher power. What will it represent to you? To what will you dedicate your practice and workouts?

Ideal State Vision

In this process, we will envision and program an ideal state for entering your workouts, which you will then be able to access with ease and in short order. First, know that any meditation done prior to your workouts will aid in creating an ideal state. This process is best executed while standing as you might be prior to entering a workout.

Find a comfortable, safe place to stand.

Close your eyes, take a deep breath in, and relax with the fall.

Imagine you have just arrived for an important workout. Take a moment to create an image. Soak in the sights and sounds, the air against your skin, whatever you are sensing, and anyone there to witness you. Pay attention to your thoughts in this environment. What kind of thoughts go through your mind? What do you feel in your heart?

Today, like every day, is important. *The workout,* and everything that goes into it, matters. You want to do well in life and in this workout, and that is okay. It is okay to admit these vulnerabilities to ourselves.

After arriving, you go through your warm-up and prepare your body for what is to come. This is your ritual, a ritual that varies day to day based on the karma of prior workouts, any tightness or soreness, and in specifically preparing for the demands of today's *lifts* and *movements.*

At just the right time, you pause and close your eyes for an extended blink, standing right where you are. Both in the vision and right now physically, take a deep breath in, and as you do, allow your hands with your palms facing up to rise along with the rise of your breath. As you exhale, turn your hands gracefully palms down and lower them with the fall of your breath. This can be a powerful *anchor* and conductor of intention. As you do this, focus on relaxing and preparing to enter *the workout* with your energy flowing smoothly. With each breath, gather strength. Bring yourself into the presence of strength, steadily breathing. Your lungs are delivering oxygen. Your mind and body are relaxed yet alert, focused, and ready for action. Your muscles are relaxed yet ready to fire and work together.

Surrender any resistance for what you are about to do. If there is any nervous energy, harness and filter it through your heart, helping to open your heart and increase mental focus. Nerves mean it is important, significant, and it matters. From here on, any nerves will only serve to remind you to engage your heart, relax, and prepare yourself.

Still in this extended blink before going into action, release any heavy energy and breathe in light energy, creating a lightness of being and lightness afoot. You are ready to move. You can't wait to move. You know what is about to take place. You are about to go into action. You are preparing yourself, and you are ready to lean in to *the challenge*. You know that when you open your eyes, you will be in a place of strength and power to *lift*, move, and exert yourself. You are aligned with inner strength, and you are happy. Your entire body and being say "bring it on." This is going to be fun. This is an opportunity.

Your eyes open in the vision and you are ready to move and go. See yourself take off into *the workout*, and when you are ready, bring yourself back to where you now stand, fully present, and open your eyes.

Prepare to Move

In this process, similar to entering an ideal state, you will prepare yourself for movement in a *meditative state*. This is a short and simple practice to enhance performance.

Begin seated on the edge of your seat with your feet planted. Take a deep breath in, and relax with the fall.

While flowing with your breath, bring your awareness to your forehead. Imagine a line through the middle of your brain, and sense your brainwaves slowing to the perfect level. What does pinpoint focus and *pure intention* feel like from this place? Set this pinpoint focus on what is about to take place. Stand up and further prepare yourself for movement. Envision the *movement* and how you will engage it. Allow the intention of your gaze to symbolize your intention of executing. You are ready to move. Take a deep energy-gathering breath, fully present and focused, and go!

A Meditative Squat

This is a brief meditation at the bottom position of a squat that can be incorporated into your daily warm-up. When you rest at the bottom of a squat, as upright as possible, it is similar to a seated meditative posture.

Find a comfortable place to stand.

Go into your best squat – with your feet around shoulder-width apart, squeeze your glutes and sink straight down into those muscles, all the way to the bottom, with relaxed quads, active glutes, your knees out over your toes, your weight toward your heels, hips open, chest up, back straight, and rear-end as close to your ankles as possible. Tune in to your energy and breathing.

Practice entering a *meditative state*. From here, you can shift your balance to stretch your ankles. To help open your hips, you can push your knees out with your elbows while your hands are together prayer-like. Whatever you choose to do, focus your will and hold the posture until you decide to rest, at which point slide a yoga block or foam roller underneath you, and sit in a seated squat posture. Close your eyes and continue the meditation, aligning for *the workout*. This is your practice, and from here, you may flow with it wherever it takes you. Meditate like this for however long as you like, and you can also repeat in repetitions.

A Meditative Hold

Similar to a meditative squat, a meditative hold is a simple process that applies to any type of hold, such as a plank, the support position on the rings, hanging from a high bar, holding a barbell overhead or in a front-racked squat, a handstand, a yoga posture, or sitting upright with a straight spine. Whenever we hold a position, it is meditative in nature and provides the opportunity for *pure intention*. As a note, processes of this nature help to transfer a *meditative state* to *movements* and *lifts* in *the workout*.

For this example, you will be hanging from a pull-up bar, however, you may substitute a hold of your choice.

Once you have found an apparatus to conduct your practice, close your eyes, take a deep breath in, and relax with the fall. Spend a moment setting the intention for what you are about to do. In just a moment, not yet, but in just a moment, you will open your eyes, jump up, and hang from the bar or rings for as long as you can, a max effort hold.

Open your eyes, look up to spot the apparatus, and jump (or step up) to the bar. Find a comfortable grip. It is okay to adjust your grip or move about at any time. As you hang there, bring your awareness to the way you are hanging. Notice there are different ways to hang and different muscles that can be engaged. Notice what feels best and resonates strength.

Bring your awareness to your breath. Focus on taking smooth, calming, oxygenating breaths. Close your eyes and continue to breathe. Tune in to every sensation. Imagine your energy flowing upward. Practice creating a feeling of lightness. Continue to breathe. Soon this will be a matter of heart and mind over body, a test of will. See how long you can maintain a powerful, positive state of engagement, one of *pure intention*, determination, and strength. What will motivate you to keep going when it gets hard? What is within you? Continue to hold until you choose to let go.

Meditative Stretching

It is highly beneficial to develop the habit of mobilizing throughout your day as well as before, during, and after your workouts. Developing your mobility practice is one of the best things you can do for the health of your joints and tissues, as well as for your overall fitness. It also provides the opportunity or reminder to pause for a meditative moment. It is a process of working with your body, working on tight areas, working on areas causing pain or discomfort, rehabilitating trouble spots, and changing the story of your body. Strong muscles are both powerful and supple, able to reach full ranges of motion. Muscles and joints without full range of motion are more vulnerable to injury. There are different kinds of strength, and there is always something that can humble us. Mobility work can be a humbling practice. This process works well with a combination of yoga postures, static holds, and dynamic stretching. The contrast of dynamic and static stretching mirrors active and passive meditation.

Find a good space to do some meditative stretching.

Close your eyes, take a deep breath in, and relax with the fall.

Open your eyes and begin with any stretch of your choice.

As you go into it, breathe into the location that is being stretched. Relax into it. Pause, relax, then stretch deeper. Relax into the sensation. Move to look for the stretch in different ways, and continue to breathe.

Each stretch and posture can carry intention. Reach up to the sky and allow joy to descend from above. Reach down to the floor with the intention of grounding. Release energy in between stretches. Open your mouth wide to create tension, then release the energy in your neck and face. Stretch your upper abs and chest with the intention of opening your heart. This is your practice, and you may do with it and create what you will.

Tune in to your body and recent *fitness karma*. Listen for where to flow next. This is an intuitive practice. Continue to breathe into the stretch and into the area of focus. At any time, you can pause and close your eyes, further cultivating a *meditative state* with intention, presence, and awareness. Work with your energy and your breath as you mobilize your body. If there is anywhere that needs extra care, work the entire chain up and down from the area, and be sure to balance both sides of your body.

If this is part of your warm-up, trust your knowing for when you are ready for *the workout*.

Meditative Mobility

This process is focused on myofascial release and further cultivating meditative elements into your mobility work. You will need a foam roller, a massage ball (preferably five inches in diameter), or another mobility tool of choice. The formula is to enter a *meditative state*, then breathe and relax into the muscle being worked, tuning in and listening to your body, releasing energy, and flowing through your mobility practice.

Find a good space to conduct your mobility practice.

Close your eyes, take a deep breath in, and relax.

With each relaxing breath, tune in to your body and recent *fitness karma*. Tune in to the flow of energy throughout your body. Where will you begin your practice? What area of your body will you work on? What area will help unlock other areas? What systems need extra love and care?

When you are ready, open your eyes and begin your practice with your roller at your chosen location. Slowly roll into the tissue, pausing to breathe and relax on any tight spots or trigger points. Let the roller sink into the tissue as you relax the area. Whenever you catch yourself wincing or tightening, especially your face, take a deep breath, relax, and send relaxation with your breath to the area you are working on. Imagine yourself flooding this area with clean and clear oxygen and energy. Periodically close your eyes for an extended blink. Set the intention of releasing energy around the area along with the physical release taking place. With acute awareness, pay attention to what you feel taking place. Notice when you feel any changes within the tissue. Notice when you feel a dispersion or release, when you feel the roller sink deeper into the tissue. Notice when to move on, slowly working your way through your body.

When you finish, stand up and move around. Test the areas worked and your flow of energy; focus on feeling the difference. Now is the perfect time for any length of sitting practice.

Find a comfortable place to sit.

Close your eyes and spend some time enjoying the benefits of your mobility work: increased relaxation, a better flow of energy, endorphins, and everything else. Pay attention to all the sensations. You may find that you are better able to work with your energy or carry out other intentions within yourself.

There are many complements to go along with your mobility practice. Among these are clean foods, proper hydration, and meditation. Mobility soft-tissue work encourages you to be more conscious of the food and water you put in your body. Both make a difference in your tissue. Make a habit out of drinking water before and after soft-tissue work, and as you do so, place some meditative intention with the water to aid the release.

Seeing the Workout

This is a vision process of going through a workout, a practice of creating success in preparation. To do this process, you will either need to have a particular workout in mind or create one as you go. Often, when you know what you are about to do in a workout, this happens naturally. However, you want to be conscious of what you are envisioning and align with strength and success. This can happen in an instant with your eyes open or closed any time prior to, or even during, *the workout.*

For now, find a comfortable place to sit or stand.

Close your eyes, take a deep breath in, and relax with the fall.

As you breathe in, focus on how the air fills your diaphragm and lungs. Focus on feeling the energy of your body. Notice any vibrations that are present, simply paying attention and coming into greater presence.

On your next breath, breathe and flow to the area of your forehead; bring into your mind's eye the journey of *the workout* upon which you are about to embark. How will you choose to see yourself? What is the first *lift, movement,* or *skill?* Go through it and see yourself executing. From there, move on to the next *movement* and envision the way you want to engage your workout. See yourself engaging from a place of strength with consistent exertion of power and energy. Go through each *movement.* See yourself moving well and executing with perfect form. Envision the rhythm of the *movement.* Notice how everything feels just right, how your body and the weights feel lighter when all of the best muscles are recruited for the job. Within the vision, notice your breathing and the way your heart is beating. Envision the *movements* with their corresponding breaths. Envision when to take your rests, when you may need them. Envision yourself working with deep, smooth, relaxing breaths, helping to calm your heart rate and steadily deliver oxygen, equaling more efficient recovery and shorter rests. For workouts with a time component, know that you have exactly enough time to do what you are capable of doing. See yourself flow through *the workout.*

Continue to create a vision of *the workout* you want. Practice envisioning it the way you want to engage it. See yourself hitting new personal records, pushing yourself, maximizing your effort, working hard for something greater than your smaller self. Visions of this nature can happen in a moment, but you can also spend as much time as you like creating these images of successful engagement. You can envision it quickly with broad brushstrokes or you can go through it slowly and in detail. You can envision it as though looking at yourself, or you can envision it as though you are in it, seeing through your own eyes. You can even mimic the *movements* with little micro movements, mentally rehearsing *skills* and *lifts.* This is your practice, and it is unique to you.

When you see yourself finish *the workout,* what do you see yourself doing? How do you feel? What is your state of being? How does your body feel? Notice your breathing and heart rate calming down, returning to normal. Still in the vision, take a look around. Where would you like to go to stretch, meditate, and enjoy these moments? What space invites you? Go there now to stretch, sit, and meditate. How does it feel to meditate after this physical exertion? What does it feel like to elevate your state of being and bask in the endorphins and the moment, to connect with all that is going on in your body? Stay here for as long as you like; this is what waits for you in your next meditative workout.

When you are ready, bring yourself back to where you are with a deep grounding breath, fully present and awake, and open your eyes.

Breaking Limitations

Similar to seeing *the workout,* this process is about seeing yourself set new personal records, going past what you previously thought possible, seeing yourself lift a heavier weight, make a certain time, run faster, jump higher, or complete more reps. This could be anything that exceeds what you thought was possible for you, and it can also apply to health and body-related beliefs. To do this process, you will need to have in mind one or more *lifts* or *movements* with which to see yourself break prior limits.

Find a comfortable place to sit or stand.

Close your eyes, take a deep breath, and relax.

Take a moment to identify any limitations you place on yourself in relation to your workouts or your life. What do you believe is possible for you? In what areas do you not believe you can do something? What limits do you place on yourself or your life? These might be subconscious beliefs that need to rise to the surface. Look at areas of your life you would like to improve. Take as long as you need to identify and make these connections.

You are approaching the time to shatter your limits.

Pull up a vision of a specific *lift* or *movement* for which you will set a new personal record. Pay attention to the way you feel as you imagine yourself approaching it. Do you believe you can break this record? Are there any doubts present? How do you overcome your doubts and fears? What needs to be done for you to break this limit? How do you see yourself do it? Can you see all the work that has been put in to get here? All the workouts, the practice, the changes, and new healthy habits? Can you see the karma, everything clicking, coming together to make it happen, falling into place?

The time has come. This is your time, and you are ready.

Step into yourself. See the vision from within yourself, through your own eyes. It doesn't matter what you have or haven't done before. These moments have never happened before. You step up without hesitation, but rather *pure intention* in your gaze. Whatever you are about to do, notice what you see, hear, touch, and feel. If it is a *lift*, notice how the bar feels in your hands. Notice what your body feels like in motion and the way the ground feels under your feet. Notice the state of strength you are in as you know you are about to shatter this limit. In a moment, you will know it is time to pull the trigger.

At just the right time, you go for it. Feel, see, and hear yourself break your limits, executing the *lift, movement, skill,* or workout, beyond anything you have ever done, beyond what you thought you were capable. Will you allow yourself to be surprised? If it is a long-term process, see it in fast-forward. Keep going until you know you have done it.

When you are on the other side, step into how it feels. What does it mean for you to have done this, to have believed in yourself? Take a few moments to soak this in. How does this help you in other areas of your life?

You can repeat this process regularly to keep yourself moving toward your dreams. Every day is an opportunity to break free of limiting beliefs. For now, when you are ready, fully present and awake, open your eyes.

Becoming Lighter

This is a practice of becoming lighter in spirit and on your feet. With *pure intention*, focus on clearing heavy energy and feeling lighter with bounce and spring in your step. Regardless of your size or weight, it is about the way you feel in relation to yourself.

Step One: Close your eyes and take a moment to relax with *pure intention*.

Step Two: Open your eyes and begin to bounce up and down without leaving the ground. Do this by slightly bending at your knees, then springing up on your toes. Repeat this and observe how light or heavy you feel. Next, jump slightly off the ground and again observe how it feels.

Step Three: Close your eyes, and with each breath, practice making yourself lighter using any method of your choosing. Imagine your energy flowing upward; gather any heavy energy and release it with your exhale; spin or float your energy up; breathe up and down your body and spine, flowing with your energy from your feet to your head and beyond; send energy out through your hands and feet with the *pure intention* of becoming lighter; repeat to yourself, "I am becoming lighter with each breath, each moment lighter and lighter."

Step Four: Begin rolling up on your toes again and notice any difference in the weight of your energy. Begin bouncing slightly off the ground from the balls of your feet, feeling lighter and lighter, as if you could jump your highest at any moment. Allow the right muscles to help you create a spring in your step. Continue this process until you feel yourself lighter.

Repeat these steps as needed, and each time you do, go deeper within yourself, deeper within your ability. It is about practice.

For a variation, try the *becoming lighter shuffle*. Begin by gently bouncing on the balls of your feet. Shuffle and glide your feet back and forth. When your left foot comes to center, your right foot goes out, then comes back, and the left foot goes out, so your feet are shuffling back and forth in unison. As you do this, practice becoming lighter, feeling yourself floating above the ground, completely relaxed except for the muscles powering the *movement*. Let go of any heavy energy as you shuffle, relaxing your shoulders and arms, shaking out any tension in your body. You can exaggerate the bounce for just this purpose, with your shoulders and arms bouncing along with your body, relaxing any tension, releasing any weight, simply loose, relaxed, and light.

A Meditative Walk

A meditative walk can be a simple part of your daily practice. The walk is a process similar to *the workout* and can transfer over into it. A walk has a clear start and clear end, providing the opportunity to go from here to there. A meditative walk helps raise your state of being. What will you create? What intention will you set? What question will you pose for clarity? Prior to and during your walk, close your eyes for some relaxing breaths. Enter a *meditative state*; increase inner and outer awareness; survey your inner world; and bring yourself into presence.

Be sure you are in a safe place and aware of your surroundings.

Begin walking with a peaceful stride, periodically pausing to close your eyes and breathe. Close your eyes for a few paces, not long, but just right for the purpose of your meditative walk. With each step, relax and align with your intention. Focus on your breathing and continue relaxing in mind and body. As you walk, imagine yourself floating across the ground. Imagine what it would be like to walk on a cloud. Open your eyes, still floating and gliding, nurturing a deeper level of mind. Allow whatever is happening within you to happen. You can clear spaces, clear energy, and dance in your soul as you walk. Imagine yourself floating up and out of your body, flying above. Imagine yourself floating above, sitting in meditation while you walk. These are some of the things you can do with a meditative walk, and you can be creative in your inner world to create vibrant energy, love, peace, and joy. This is where you practice being happy and connect with soul bliss.

When distractions arise in meditation or a meditative walk, we have two good options. We may remain in the meditation and allow it to mirror the distractions of life, learning any lessons we can. Or we can come out of it, address the distraction, invite laughter and joy, patience and serenity, and then return to the meditation, going deeper in the matter of a moment.

Walking Lighter

This is a specific process of walking lighter, which can also be applied to running or bodyweight *movements* in *the workout*.

Find a clear space to conduct your walk.

With your eyes open, envision a space of approximately 10 paces that you will walk with your eyes closed. Imagine stepping into uncharted territory in your life. Begin walking, and after a couple of steps, close your eyes and continue to envision and walk the space and distance.

You are enhancing your inner focus and vision. As you do this, take deep relaxing breaths and connect with your flow of energy. Move your consciousness and energy to your legs and feet. Focus on each leg and foot as it rises and falls with each step. Create an upward flow of energy in unison with your exhale. Imagine your energy flowing up from your feet as each one rises and falls, one step after another. Create the sensation of walking lightly, floating across the ground. As you do this, make subtle adjustments in the way you walk to contribute to the lightness. This includes the angle of your body, the strike of your foot, and the muscles in your legs. You are relaxed, tuned in, and aided by your breath. Open your eyes when you feel as though you have reached the distance you envisioned in your mind. Continue to walk a similar distance, then close your eyes again and repeat the process. Continue to practice becoming lighter.

For an added bonus and alternative, practice counting your steps with your eyes closed, at a deeper state of being.

Creating Strength

Some days we feel stronger than others, and we often feel stronger as *the workout* progresses, which is a common phenomena as blood flow increases to the muscles. The intention for this process is for you to take ownership, so that you feel stronger more often, and on days when you feel weak, you can do something about it to put yourself in a state of strength, working with your energy to create strength. There are many different ways to do this, and a process such as this can be done in the warm-up or at any point throughout *the workout.*

Find a good place to stand.

Close your eyes, take a deep breath in, and relax.

On your next inhale, gather your strength and energy. Allow it to reside within you. Repeat this process, imagining yourself gathering all of your strength, growing stronger with each breath. If there is any energy of weakness, acknowledge and release it; imagine strength coming in, filling you up, drowning out and overcoming the weak energy. This is not about resisting weakness (resistance is a weak position), but about embracing strength and all else. Imagine weak energy dissolving into strength. Imagine that one of your hands represents the weak energy and the other hand represents strength, and then bring them together, collapsing and uniting. Repeat this as needed. You are balancing and aligning with strength. You are thinking strong, feeling strong, and breathing strong. Set a reminder for this state. What will help trigger this strength within you? As always, this is your chance to build your own practice. Be creative. You can choose to create strength in ways that work for you. When you have created a state of strength, open your eyes.

Dance Vision

This vision is about seeing yourself dancing and breaking free of barriers. It is about connecting with soul presence, being true to yourself, and letting go of image. It is about having fun and allowing yourself to move freely and enjoy *the workout*.

Find a good place to sit or stand.

Close your eyes, take a deep breath, and relax.

Allow yourself to create a vision in your heart. You are standing on a beautiful stage, looking out on a full crowd. This is a time where you must dance in front of a great number of onlookers. Notice who is in the crowd, those you love, those who love you, and the world at large. The instructions are simple: Be yourself and express yourself through movement.

The perfect song begins. You close your eyes, open your heart, and focus on feeling the music. Stirring your heart, it comes alive within you. You can't help but start to move with the beat. Perhaps it's your foot that begins to tap, or your head or hand, slowly at first. Notice how this begins for you. How much will you hold yourself back or how much will you let yourself go? What would you do if you were completely free? How would you move? How grandiose, how graceful, or how subtle? This is your expression. Your fingerprint is in your walk, your breath, your movement, and your dance. The music builds, still moving through you, and you let go. Anything that was holding you back is now gone. You have extended beyond your body. Your energy radiates to the crowd with each *movement*. You are moving freely, doing what only you would do, dancing how only you would dance. Your heart is engaged and you have surrendered to the music, allowing it to guide you. Your soul is dancing. No more thinking is required. You are present in the moment. You are allowing yourself to have fun, following your bliss in the music and movement. Continue to dance until you know your dance has come to an end. Your life is the dance, and the music is in your soul.

When you are ready, you can open your eyes.

The Workout

Presence

THE FOLLOWING ARE methods of calling upon greater presence within yourself. During your workouts, take deep breaths, gather your energy within yourself, plant your feet, and connect with your faith. Allow all else to drop away – no past, no future – only the physical exertion and what it represents to you in the moment.

Open your heart for greater presence by connecting with what you feel. What is with you in your thoughts and heart? Is there anything you need to acknowledge to yourself to gain greater presence? Acknowledge and release it so that all that is left is your presence.

If you find yourself moving quickly on the inside, relax and slow within yourself. If your eyes lose focus, bring them back into focus. If your mind wanders or you find yourself distracted, bring yourself back into presence with the task at hand. Lean in and give yourself to the moments of your training. Make a difference with your presence.

Hypnotic Counting

This is a process of counting repetitions with *pure intention*, a vision of *the workout*, planting the seed to keep going, where the counting is all there is. You will need to have in mind a *lift* or *movement* of which you would like to be able to do many repetitions – pushups, pull-ups, squats, or anything else you choose. In what is about to follow, envision yourself completing each rep. See how much fun it can be to simply count your repetitions. These prostrations are a symbol of your devotion and dedication. Count them with this in your heart.

Find a comfortable place to sit or stand.

Close your eyes, take a deep breath, and relax.

It is time to create a vision of *the workout* where you will complete as many reps as possible. Where will you do this work? What do you feel as you are about to test yourself? Envision yourself approaching the space to conduct this practice, and prepare yourself to begin. You are in position; the clock signals go with a long beep. You begin counting with each completed rep – 1, 2, 3, it's very easy to start, 4, 5, 6, feeling good, 7, 8, 9, your reps become more efficient with each count, 10, 11, 12. You are determined to keep counting. All you are focused on is counting each rep, 13, 14, 15, 16, and all you want to do is keep counting, 17, 18, 19. If there is any part of you that wants to slow down, you overtake that with the part of you that loves counting, 20, 21, 22, 23. Keep counting, 24, 25, 26. You're reaching a new personal record, going beyond any number you've done before. There is something special about counting this far, but it doesn't matter, you simply have the desire to keep counting, 27, 28, 29, 30, and all of a sudden you are counting faster than before, 31, 32, 33, seeming to know that you have two options: either quit or count faster. So you count faster, 34, 35, 36, 37, 38, 39, 40, until you decide to stop and rest for the next time you get to count again.

Take a deep breath, bring yourself back, 1, 2, 3, and open your eyes.

Rest Periods

This practice is about the rest and recovery time during your workouts. These short *rest periods* are ideal meditative opportunities. This is where you gather yourself, enter an ideal state of recovery, settle your breathing, bathe your body with oxygen, and recharge your energy. This is where you tap into your nervous system and aid the processes of your body. What we don't want is hyperactive, shallow breathing, as though in a frenzy or panic, with tight muscles and friction in your mind. With meditation, you learn to relax at the height of intensity and recover more quickly.

These periods could be the result of maximum effort, pushing to the point that you must rest. They could be the result of temporary muscle failure, or they could simply be the *rest periods* in between sets of *lifts*. They can last anywhere from a few seconds to a couple of minutes before going back to work. These moments are where you reap the benefits of your practice, the art of relaxation, becoming *the breath,* tuning in to *the body,* expanding awareness, creating greater presence, *pure intention,* focusing your thoughts, opening your heart and lungs. All of this merges together in these precious moments. This is where your practice leads to optimal performance. *The practice* is to enter a *meditative state* of relaxed recovery, to remain loose and fluid with the intention of recovering more quickly. We all have our own levels of fitness; this practice helps us to maximize our potential and rise in our individual level.

From wherever you are in your workout, when it is time for rest and recovery, take a deep breath in, pause for a split-second at the top, and release with a smooth, relaxing exhale. As you do this, calm and recharge your energy. Flow with the energy of your breath, releasing the sensations of exertion. As your breathing relaxes, continue taking deep, smooth breaths with the intention of sending oxygen where it is needed. Imagine your muscles bathing in oxygen, soaking up all of it. On your exhales, imagine lactic acid flushing out along with the carbon dioxide in your exhales. Shake your arms and legs, and bounce up and down with the firm intention of relaxing your muscles. Set the intention that your muscles are recovering, that your full strength is returning. Let out a fun sound that also symbolizes releasing sensations. If you drink water during your *rest*, add an appropriate intention to the water and continue to align with your highest potential.

Jumping-Jack Calm-Down

Building on *rest periods,* this is a process to practice calming your heart rate and breathing. It involves three successive rounds of 20 jumping-jacks, followed by closing your eyes and practicing the three different phases. Feel free to substitute other *movements.* This can be great with sprints or any heart-pumping exercise. The main purpose is to go through the different rounds and develop your practice.

Upon completion of the jumping-jacks, close your eyes and tune in to your body, primarily through your heartbeat, pulse, and breathing. Tune in to every detail, all the sensations throughout your body. Pay attention to your heart rate, any pulses you feel, and the speed and depth at which you are breathing. At the same time, access a deeper part of mind, slowing to a perfect brainwave.

Round 1: Complete 20 quality jumping-jacks. Close your eyes, and with a natural breath, simply observe everything that is happening within you as your body returns to a resting state. Focus on feeling and observing all the sensations – your heartbeat, breathing, and anything else. You are allowing all of it to take place.

Round 2: Complete 20 perfect jumping-jacks. Close your eyes, and now alter your breath with the intention of slowing your heart rate. Take deep, smooth, relaxing breaths as you return to a normal state of rest.

Round 3: Complete 20 jumping-jacks. Close your eyes, and now tap into your entire system. Tune in to your spine and central nervous system. Focus your attention on the area from your brain to the back of your neck and length of your spine. Focus on calming the energy running along your spine, absorbing the energy of your breath to help. Focus on relaxing your heart and lungs. Relax it all and return to a resting state.

You can repeat these rounds using a lesser number of repetitions to continue to train your body to listen to higher self.

Forgiveness and Gratitude

This is a practice of forgiveness and gratitude as you journey through your workouts. Close your eyes and spend some sincere time with these questions: How do you feel toward yourself and your body? What kind of communication do you offer yourself and your body? How would you like to treat yourself and your body? If there are any parts of your body you don't like, then those are areas to focus on and create greater harmony. You can step toward love and gratitude in any moment.

In addition to your thoughts and attitude, this is about forgiving yourself for doing things that you know haven't been good for you, such as eating poorly, being "out of shape," not exercising, not stretching or doing your mobility work, not drinking enough water, not getting enough sleep, or any number of other things unique to you. This is also an opportunity to forgive your body, troublesome joints, old injuries, or any parts of your body you have harbored ill-will toward.

The workout is the perfect opportunity to practice this forgiveness and gratitude. Think about everything your body allows you to do. When your legs, arms, hands, and shoulders are burning in *the workout*, tell them how much you love them, and forgive yourself for eating poorly or anything else you need to forgive yourself for. "I love you, legs and feet. I love you, knees and elbows. I love you, hands and arms. I love you, heart and lungs. I forgive you for any pain and challenges you've given me, and I forgive myself for not taking better care of you."

In those moments of physical exertion, experiencing all the accompanying physical sensations, forgive yourself and others, your body and body parts, and ask for forgiveness in return. Silently repeat, whisper, or declare aloud to yourself and your body, "I forgive you, (self). I forgive you for (this or that). I forgive you, (body). I forgive you, (body part). I'm grateful for you, (body). Forgive me for (having done this or that)."

Allow this practice to lead to gratitude. See how it feels to be grateful for what you are doing in the moment, engaging in an act of love, and doing all of this good for yourself.

Embrace the Challenge

This is a simple process of surrendering and embracing *the challenge*, your inner attitude toward the engagement.

Close your eyes and ask yourself, "What am I resisting? What within myself do I need to surrender to?" We often resist what we perceive to be negative, and we surrender to these things in order to transform them.

Imagine yourself embracing all challenges. What does this look like for you? What thoughts do you have in doing so? What do you feel in your heart in doing so? Imagine yourself leaning in rather than shying away. What does this give you on the inside?

In true surrender, we don't even resist any resistance we may feel. Surrender to how you feel, surrender to the sensations that are happening. If you are resisting anything, surrender to whatever you are resisting. Let yourself see and feel all of it; experience your truth and find your power.

Executing the Lift

Nothing induces meditation quite like staring at a barbell in preparation for a big *lift*. This process is about the physics and metaphysics of *the body* in action. Rather than make ourselves light, here is where we want to make ourselves tight, heavy, and sturdy while making the weight feel lighter. When executing a *lift* or *movement,* you want to feel the simplest, most efficient way of executing. It is up to you to develop the feeling of when you are executing properly from a position of strength and safety. Rather than thinking your way through it, tap into your intuitive athleticism. We want to transcend the act of thinking to execute in a fluid, athletic manner. When executing properly, based on your form, recruiting the larger, primary muscles needed, the *lift* feels easier. This is the feeling for you to seek out, feeling it happening with more ease.

While this is a process to put into action, here is a vision for what that might look like using the example of a weightlifting meet. When you do it for yourself, feel free to envision your own sport, *lift*, or *movement.*

Close your eyes, take a deep breath, and relax within.

Allow yourself to create a vision in your heart and mind.

Imagine stepping onstage to execute either a max deadlift, snatch, or clean and jerk. You have already warmed-up, and you now have one minute for the lift. You step up and focus all of your attention on the barbell. With the intention of your walk and your gaze, you put yourself in a place where there is no hesitation. It is just you and the barbell, and you know it is going up, nothing but *pure intention.* Everything you do has purpose. You take two deep breaths, gathering strength, and grounding to the platform. You are one with the platform, one with the barbell. You have practiced this *lift.* You don't need to think about all the details or nuances in the *movement.* You only need to match your vibration to your perfect execution. Your body knows what to do. You know how it feels. How do you see yourself go through your own pre-lift routine? What do you do that is unique to you? After the two deep breaths, you take two big steps and plant your feet while your hands plant on the bar. Meanwhile, your eyes don't move from the bar until you look up, in position, with all the right muscles engaged, solid as a rock. Then, with a final belly breath, without thinking, you begin to pull the bar with *pure intention*. Everything else follows. You maintain your center and balance that emanates from your straight spine, aided by your breath. With fluidity and no wasted movement, you instinctively know what to do to execute, feeling the rhythm of the *lift* and the leverage that your body creates. You feel strong at every phase, always in a secure position with the best muscles being recruited, confidently completing the *lift* as an extension of your will.

Spend as long as you like creating a vision of your perfect execution, and when you are ready, take a deep breath, and open your eyes.

Workout Mantras

For a simple and powerful application, repeat a mantra or affirmation while going through your workouts. Think about what you are creating for yourself, your heart, and your life. Connect the words with intention and heart. Make it personal, and make it matter to you. What do you want to affirm for yourself? For your heart, mind, body, and soul? Ask yourself what would serve your highest good. As you go through your workout, repeat your chosen affirmation, and observe what happens within yourself.

For more on mantras and affirmations, including examples, see the short section at the end of these processes.

Opposing Forces

This process is designed to help you make new connections and create new awareness for whenever you slip into unconscious negative thoughts. The process consists of two rounds of physical exertion that can be repeated multiple times for greater impact and further light bulbs.

For the first round, as you go through a *lift* or *movement*, repeat a negative statement such as, "I can't do it" or, "I quit." If you want to make an even greater impact on your subconscious, say it in a silly way, such as a high-pitched voice, and listen to how funny you sound when you say it.

For the second round, with the same *movement*, repeat a positive statement such as, "I am doing it" or, "I can do this forever." Bring your awareness to what comes up within you. A simple process such as this has the potential to bring about significant realizations.

Silence

This process can be done individually or as a group for a more powerful effect. If done in a group, it would be done in waves or heats.

Pick a bodyweight *movement* such as squats or burpees.

Round 1: Complete as many reps as possible for one minute in complete silence. Observe and face what comes up within you. Observe your energy. Focus on generating your own energy and finding peace in the exertion. Upon completing the round, rest for two minutes in silence.

Round 2: Complete as many reps as possible in one minute while being vocal, letting out noises with your breath, grunting, whatever is natural to you. Play music, and if there are others present, have them provide encouragement — real, heartfelt cheers, shouts, and claps.

Repeat this process and look for new realizations about the way you engage. Silence can magnify your inner world. Rather than looking for what you already know, look for new connections within yourself, your heart, and in sensing energy from beyond yourself.

Post-Workout

Post-workout is one of the most beneficial and beautiful times to sit for some precious moments. Like lying in savasana at the end of a yoga session, even two to five minutes can help calm your nervous system.

In these sacred post workout moments, you can tap into love, peace, joy, gratitude, and other feelings of soul bliss. You can *go in* and simply observe the sensations of your body after the exertion, which will undoubtedly be different than at other times. Tune in to your chest and lungs. Feel your heart open wide. Tune in to your vibration, which you are better able to sense at these times after cellular activation.

If you are experiencing tightness anywhere in your body, practice relaxing, releasing, and clearing the energy. Combine this practice with your mobility work. Triggers that lead to these post-workout meditations can include stretching, foam rolling, taking a shower, drinking water, and preparing your post-workout nourishment. You can take a moment to close your eyes and breathe and relax your nervous system wherever you are. You can use this sacred time in a variety of ways, from recovering to simply enjoying the rewards of your efforts.

Recovery

This is an example of a post-workout recovery meditation. You may also apply other practices to your recovery that you've been developing.

Find a place to sit, stand, or lie down in a neutral position. Close your eyes, take a deep breath, and relax.

Focus on calming your nervous system by breathing up and down your spine with soothing breaths. Bring your awareness to the energy that has been created by *the workout*. Notice any lingering vibrations throughout your body, and use these sensations to help you relax.

Bring your consciousness to any tight areas that need to be released. With *pure intention*, imagine breathing through those parts of your body, so the energy breathes and flows in and out from those locations, cleansing your field of space, until you feel a shift or release.

Focus on feeling the cells of your body. Imagine resting at the center of every cell. Allow relaxation to wash over you. Allow yourself to enter a blissful state. Tune in to the endorphins that have been released, reflect on the heart and energy that was poured into *the workout*, the challenges encountered and overcome, the successes and accomplishments. Let yourself be pleased with what you just achieved.

Where are your thoughts? Are you happy with your effort and attitude? Fall into your heart and rest there for some time. How do you feel? What's in your heart?

Imagine yourself recovering well. How will you aid in this process? Will you drink plenty of clear fluids? Will you eat well? Will you sleep a deep, recovering sleep? How will you nurture the cells of your body?

You can spend as long as you like and do whatever you want while in this state. This is your time, and when you are finished, bring yourself back, open your eyes, give yourself a little stretch, shake out your arms and legs, and drink some more water.

Oxygen Flood Release

Close your eyes, take a deep breath, and relax.

Begin by flooding your body with oxygen through smooth, slightly accelerated, deep breaths. *The breath* is the key. Use full lung capacity and take in more oxygen than you need in your current resting state.

After a few moments, you will begin to feel the vibration that accompanies this type of breathing. Using that vibration, send oxygen and energy to your brain, nervous system, and any other areas that need it. Practice magnifying the vibration to accelerate healing and relaxation. Enhance your awareness of what you are capable of within your body. You can either magnify or stop the vibration with your intention and allowing. Focus on your central nervous system and the energy that flows along your spine. Focus on feeling your energy flowing more readily. Tap into your central nervous system, which has already been activated. It can now be better utilized as one of your greatest allies in meditation.

From here, you can perform any number of small miracles within yourself. From here, you can send oxygen and healing energy anywhere in your body. This is your inner work, the work of your inner knowing.

Bathe in the oxygen and vibration. This process can be used to cleanse and clear energy, to release knots and tired energy, to sharpen your mind, and oxygenate your body and muscles.

This process of deep accelerated breathing has similar vibrational effects as chanting, and it can be done in a variety of ways. Once the initial flood of oxygen takes place, you may resume normal breathing and go back to flooding as desired.

Shower Meditation

We all need to take a shower after our workouts, which provides the perfect opportunity for a brief shower meditation. While you are in the shower, add intention to the water and allow it to shower over you. Imagine the water cleansing you inside and out, cleansing your soul, washing away worries, washing away the past and the future, leaving you only with presence in the unknown, present with possibility. Allow it to cleanse and wash away anything that needs to be washed away. Imagine the top of your head opening and the water pouring into you. With the intention of love in the water, allow love to flow within and all over you, filling you up inside. Continue with whatever else you want the water to represent.

For an added bonus, imagine the water transforming into the colors of the chakras: red, orange, yellow, green, blue, fuchsia, indigo, purple, and pure, white light. Go through them one at a time, spending time in the corresponding region, being showered with red, pouring into and all over you, resting at the base of your spine. Imagine the center of this energy expanding and engulfing you, representing firmness of purpose, new beginnings, and security. It is up to you to connect with what these mean to you in your life. Imagine orange pouring into and over you, resting your awareness below your belly button, expanding from a small center to a large sphere of energy, representing joy, balanced pleasure, and healthy sexual expression. Next, imagine yellow washing over you, filling you up, resting above your belly button, balancing your personal power, flowing with life. You hold your power, simply residing with peace within yourself no matter what is happening around you. Next, imagine green flooding within and over you, resting at your heart center, embracing the truth of how you feel, opening your heart, expanding and encompassing, flowing upward. Imagine blue pouring into the top of your head, resting at your throat, expanding in self expression, speaking your truth, being true to yourself. Next, the water turns to fuchsia, resting at your forehead, expanding and engulfing you. Allow yourself to see with Divine vision, to see the highest vision of your life. Next, imagine a Divine purple flushing into the crown of your head. Sense your connection with Divine energy. Lastly, allow the water to purify you as crystal clear, pure, white light. Allow this light to awaken and bless your entire being.

For a quick version, simply imagine all the colors washing over you together, balancing and aligning your energy centers. Imagine the top of your head opening again with all the colors pouring into you, helping everything within you and in your life to be in harmony. As you do this, connect with your firmness of purpose, new beginnings, fulfilling joy, flowing with life, holding your power within yourself, opening your heart to all that is good, expressing your truth in a healthy way, being true to yourself, seeing with Divine vision the path of your life, connecting with Divine energy, and resting with your faith.

Brain Activation

Close your eyes, take a deep breath, and relax.

Begin by breathing up and down your spine. When you are ready, move your consciousness to your brain and forehead. With *pure intention*, focus on lighting up your forehead and the back of your neck. Imagine little lightning bolts all throughout your brain – synapses and neurons firing. Imagine that you are making new connections and releasing connections that no longer serve you. Repeat throughout your left and right brain, middle, rear, and the base of your brain. Imagine that you are using all of your capacity for wisdom and understanding, instant intelligence. Imagine yourself using more of your brain, accessing your inner genius. Imagine the left and right hemispheres melding together as one, able to switch between left and right brain activities, between logic and creativity. Imagine lighting up your entire brain all at once; feel what it's like to do so. With each deep breath, send energy and oxygen to your brain. Notice any tingling sensations; gently embrace them, and move on.

If there are any thoughts running rampant, imagine taking an eraser and swiping them in your mind, swiping and clearing the thoughts. You can also practice spinning and swooshing the energy in and around your head – swoosh, swoosh, swoosh, as any pressure or friction in your mind clears. You can use your hands by waving them as the eraser near the sides of your head. With an appropriate intention for your mental health in this moment, gently tap your temples, forehead, cheeks, under your eyes, the back of your head, and all around.

What will you create from this state of genius within yourself? You are a clean slate. From this place of brain activation, create visions and set intentions, bringing them into your presence.

You can follow this meditation wherever it leads, and when you are ready, when your work is done for now, open your eyes.

Space Meditation

Close your eyes, take a deep breath, and relax.

Practice sensing the space in and around your body. Breathe and focus on this space, the space you fill. Sense your space within the space around you. Sense your space within all of space. Will you allow yourself to be free in this space? See if you can expand and contract, retreating to your innermost place, retreating to your spine, retreating and expanding, and then, neither, just being there, at peace in your natural space. Where does your space end and the rest of space begin? Allow your natural space to dissolve into all of space. What connections do you feel? See if you can get a sense of unity with everything inside and out. You, your space, and all of space, together as one.

There are many more things you can do with a meditation such as this. Follow the meditation for as long as you like, and when you are ready, fully present in time and space, open your eyes.

Healing

This process is intended to help promote overall health, healing, and harmonious functioning.

Close your eyes, take a deep breath, and relax.

Enter a *meditative state* and you enter a heightened state of healing. Take a moment to sit with healing energy. Bring your awareness and energy to an area that you want to promote healing. Go into the area and set the intention of healing. Clear any counter-intentions, any doubts, thoughts, or beliefs to the contrary. You can clear them in a number of creative ways. Simply acknowledging them begins the process. Acknowledge them, then wrap them up and discard them as false. Send loving and forgiving energy to the area. Believe it is possible for you and your body to miraculously heal. Believe in your body's ability to heal. You are healing. A pain that is there today can be gone tomorrow. Pain and inflammation that is here in this moment can be gone in the next. Pain can spontaneously appear and disappear. Place your hand over the area and imagine the energy flowing into your hands so you can discard it. Imagine light coming from above, flowing into you and into the area. Gently and lovingly tap the area with healing energy. Place your hand over your heart, and then move it to the area, forgiving, loving, and healing. Release any emotional weight you are carrying, and release any emotion related to the area of focus.

These are some of the innumerable ways you can promote healing within yourself. Your sincerity, vulnerability, connection, and intention make the difference. Continue to create a vibration of healing until you know you are done.

Magnification

Close your eyes, take a deep breath, and relax.

Begin with a gentle and subtle smile, first with your face and lips, then from the center of your heart. Smile in your mind;

smile with your whole body; and smile in your being. Magnify the smile and radiate this out as a pulse, smiling on the inside.

You choose what you want to feel, and when you begin to feel it, you can magnify it, whether good or bad.

What helps you connect with love? Locate a little bit of love within yourself, not someone else's, but your love. Go into the love and make it bigger. Spread love within yourself and into your life. What do you love in your life? How do you love your life? Imagine yourself emanating from the center of that love. Imagine the love growing and engulfing you, your surroundings, and expanding out to the world. You are magnifying love.

You can do this with any thought or emotion, turning it into intention and magnets. This is also how we create anxiety and other mental/emotional challenges. When you start to feel something, you can go into it further, or you can change direction and go somewhere else. You could be feeling good one moment and then choose to focus on something negative instead, arresting your happiness. How do you respond? Do you stop yourself when you get a taste of something good? Or will you stop yourself when you start spiraling downward? Make it real to you, and start with even the smallest glimmer of upliftment. With awareness and underlying intention, allow yourself to expand and magnify the positive, enlightening thoughts and emotions, engulfing all else.

Magnetization

Close your eyes, take a deep breath, and relax.

Begin by breathing up and down your spine. You are the magnet, and your spine is a magnet. Take a moment to reflect on what you are attracting in your life. What are you are currently magnetizing within yourself? And what do you want to attract in your life? Envision it now. What would you like to create? What will you magnetize within yourself right now? Take a moment. Ask your inner wisdom to help guide you, and connect with the answer in your heart.

Now focus on flowing energy up your spine. Focus your thoughts and intention, allow all molecules to align, and allow the wave of energy to work together. All is flowing together in the same direction. Sense the magnet of your spine and forehead attracting that which you are magnetizing. The magnet emanates from your center as you align the polarity of your spine. Match your vibration with what you are magnetizing.

Continue flowing upward, magnetizing your spine. Find your place of one focus and *pure intention*, magnetizing the intention. See it from the center of your forehead. Ensure your intention is pure of heart. The more open your heart, the stronger the magnetization. You are magnetizing new life for yourself.

As always, spend as long as you like in this powerful, magnetic place, and repeat regularly to institute long lasting change and to continue to attract what you want in your life.

Opening Your Heart

Close your eyes, take a deep breath, and relax.

Imagine a path that runs from your forehead to the back of your neck, down to your heart. Imagine a string that connects your head to your heart. Sometimes this string can be disconnected and needs to be repaired. This is where you do that kind of inner work.

Everything you have ever felt can be found in your heart, and you can also feel things you've never felt before. Allow your mind to help open and ping your heart. Imagine connecting the string from your head to your heart. Tune in to how you feel under the surface. What feelings do you live with on a regular basis? What small admission can you make to help open your heart? What moves you in your life? What matters to you? What do you want to feel in your heart?

Imagine a valve at the center of your chest. You control this valve, and you can open it in varying degrees. Bring your hand up and turn the valve to open, all the way open.

Lightly tap on the center of your chest with a loving intention. Use your hand to knock on the door of your heart. Are you willing to awaken your heart? Imagine yourself going through life with an open heart. What do you see yourself doing? How is your life different?

Once your heart is open, turn it upward, in a positive direction, and allow it to flow to your faith, *enlightening emotion* rather than a downward spiral. You are not here to ever wallow in anything, but to feel deeply, release, and move toward light and freedom.

Shedding Layers

Close your eyes, take a deep breath, and relax.

There are many layers to who you are, and you are about to shed layers and connect with the purity of who you are. Take a moment to consider what this means to you.

Forget what you know. Forget all that you know about yourself. Forget all the stories you tell yourself. Allow everything to fall away in these moments. With your hands, brush off your shoulders, brush off your mind, brush off your body. Can you let go of everything right now? Give yourself permission, for one moment, to let everything go. There is no past. There is no future. There is only right now. Let everything dissolve into your being, into your presence. Allow yourself to be brand new in these moments.

Imagine you have these outer layers, and you are about to step through them, and each time, you will leave these layers behind. You are no longer the person you were before. Each moment is a new moment and an opportunity for a new you.

Envision yourself shedding layers, stepping through yourself like stepping out of your clothes, stripping down to the center of being, shedding old skin. Envision your innermost self stepping through these layers. As a symbol of this, stand and take a step forward, stepping into the unknown. Leaving your old layers behind, offer them and your old self up.

Repeat this process of shedding layers and observe the shifts that happen within as you get closer to your soul perfection. Connect with the most real and true version of yourself, and enjoy every moment.

Mantras and Affirmations

MANTRAS AND AFFIRMATIONS can be used to focus thought, direct intention, and quiet your mind. They can help raise your vibration and create new patterns within yourself. When used in a repetitive nature, similar to going back to your breathing, you go back to the mantra or affirmation, continuing to repeat quietly or silently to yourself, and when you let go, you may find a space of no thought, a space of pure possibility. And if you're not quite there or if your mind wanders, you go back to the mantra or affirmation and continue to repeat it until you find yourself no longer repeating, rather simply being. Experiment with this and observe what happens in your meditation, workouts, and life. May you find results happening with ease.

Mantras are typically short but powerful expressions of heart and spirit – a sound, a word, or a short phrase that carries a vibration, where the sound and intention become one. Affirmations can be short or longer affirming statements. Both mantras and affirmations focus on creating or manifesting something in your life. You can address problems and work with your subconscious to program what you want in your life, such as, "I am creating a life I love." This is not falsely fluffing yourself up, but giving yourself permission, surrendering to your truth, and choosing better. While we are highly capable of creating the negative in our lives, we are equally capable of creating the positive. Note that for both mantras and affirmations we want to state them in the positive and in present time. We are creating what we want versus what we don't want, and we are creating it right now, not at some point in the future.

Both mantras and affirmations can be used for creating energy and anchoring states of being in *the workout*. The same way a song can remind you of a memory, a mantra or affirmation can remind you of a state of being, helping you create peak performance at any time.

To use them in *the workout*, all it takes is repeating all or part of the mantra or affirmation in a repetitive *lift* or *movement*. These could even be coach's cues to help in execution, but whatever they are, they must be what works for you, what you can believe in and align with. With each repetition and each *movement*, you are becoming one with your intention. You make the statement, "I am living my dreams." You repeat, "I love my body." You state, "These are my goals, this is my life, and it is happening," and you will know instantly at the core of being whether you believe what you are saying. This is how you know whether it is real and true right now. If you say it and you are overcome with doubts, overwhelmed at the sheer idea of it, you must shift within yourself so that when you say it, you know it is true. Your vibration matches up. You make it a reality, and you know you will take the necessary steps to reach the outcome. Remember, you don't need to know how it is going to happen, only know and believe it is already happening, and that this, right now, is part of it happening. Have faith and take steps to increase your faith. Each day is a result of where your faith resides. In chanting or repeating mantras and affirmations, focus on feeling the vibration coming from your heart.

These are my dreams, this is my life, and it is happening.

I am on my path and have been all along.

I am aligning with my path.

I am allowing all things to align.

I am creating a life I love.

I am living my dreams.

This is my life, and it is happening.

Many good things are in store.

It is all happening right now.

I love this body.

I love who I am.

Everything is okay.

Life is beautiful right now.

It is okay to be happy.

Stronger as I go.

Lighter as I go.

I am doing it.

Breath by breath.

Surrender and embrace the challenge.

I am opening my heart.

I am surrendering.

I am letting go.

I am becoming lighter in spirit.

I am love.

I am peace.

I am pure joy.

I am whole.

I can.

I am.

Om.

<u>Meditative Fitness Intentions</u>
Go inside.
Relaxed yet alert.
Slower brainwaves.
Open-hearted.
Go deeper.
Surrender.
Right now.
Envision.
Greater presence.
Expanding awareness.
Focus your thoughts.
Align in heart, mind, body, and soul.
Tune in to your body.
Become your breath.
Tap into your central nervous system.
Lightness of being.
Lightness afoot.
Strength of being.
Strength of body.
Spoken words in alignment.
Foods in alignment.
Clear, flowing energy.
Clarity of being.
Sense of well-being.
Upward flow of energy.
Embrace the challenge.
Higher performance.
Align with true strength.

Made in the USA
Charleston, SC
21 January 2016